Spilling the Script

Also from Phoenesse

AFTER THE EGO
Insights From the Pathwork® Guide
on How to Wake Up

BLINDED BY FEAR
Insights From the Pathwork® Guide
on How to Face Our Fears

WALKER
A Memoir

LIVING LIGHT
On Seeking and Finding True Faith

WORD FOR WORD
An Intimate Exchange Between a Couple of Kindred Souls
By Jill Loree and Scott Wisler

The *Real. Clear.* series offers a fresh approach to timeless spiritual teachings, conveying profound ideas by way of easier-to-read language. It's the Pathwork Guide's wisdom in Jill Loree's words.

HOLY MOLY
The Story of Duality, Darkness and a Daring Rescue

FINDING GOLD
The Search for Our Own Precious Self

BIBLE ME THIS
Releasing the Riddles of Holy Scripture

THE PULL
Relationships & Their Spiritual Significance

PEARLS
A Mind-Opening Collection of 17 Fresh Spiritual Teachings

GEMS
A Multifaceted Collection of 16 Clear Spiritual Teachings

BONES
A Building-Block Collection of 19 Fundamental Spiritual Teachings

NUTSHELLS
Snippets from *Pearls*, *Gems* and *Bones*

SPIRITUAL LAWS
Hard & Fast Logic for Forging Ahead

The *Self. Care.* How-to-Heal series offers a bird's-eye view of the Pathwork Guide's teachings and shows us how to apply them in working with others and ourselves.

SPILLING THE SCRIPT
A Concise Guide to Self-Knowing

HEALING THE HURT
How to Help Using Spiritual Guidance

DOING THE WORK
Healing Our Body, Mind & Spirit by Getting to Know the Self
By Jill Loree with Scott Wisler

www.phoenesse.com

The Guide Speaks website delivers spiritual truths by way of thousands of questions posed to the Guide and answered with candor and insight.

THE GUIDE SPEAKS
The Complete Q&A Collection
By Eva Pierrakos with Jill Loree

KEYWORDS
Answers to Key Questions
Asked of the Pathwork® Guide
By Eva Pierrakos with Jill Loree

www.theguidespeaks.com

Spilling the Script

A CONCISE GUIDE TO SELF-KNOWING

Jill Loree

Self.Care. | Book One

Published by Phoenesse LLC

www.phoenesse.com

Phoenesse® is a registered service mark of Phoenesse LLC.

ISBN-10: 0692395342

ISBN-13: 978-0692395349

"Proverbs and Tiny Songs" by Antonio Machado is taken from *The Soul Is Here For Its Own Joy*, edited and translated by Robert Bly. Copyright © 1995 by Robert Bly. Reprinted with the permission of Georges Borchardt, Inc., for Robert Bly.

Two lines from the *Magi Process* are reprinted with the permission of Jason Shulman. All copyrighted quotes and referenced material are property of their respective owners.

Pathwork® is a registered service mark owned exclusively by the Pathwork Foundation. It is used here with the permission of the Foundation. The mark may not be used without express written permission from the Pathwork Foundation.

Quotations from Pathwork® Guide Lecture Material © 2000, 2009, 2013 the Pathwork Foundation are reprinted with the permission of the Pathwork Foundation. www.pathwork.org

The ideas represented herein are the personal interpretation and understanding of the author and are not necessarily endorsed by the copyright holder of the Pathwork® Guide Lecture material.

Preface and Acknowledgments

During my four years of training to become a Pathwork Helper, I had the incredibly good fortune to be taught by a number of experienced Pathwork Helpers, many of whom had gone through decades of in-depth explorations with the Guide's teachings. Through their organizing, boiling down and sharing of these concepts, I was able to develop my own deep understanding of this profound material.

Special appreciation goes to Erena Bramos, Jack Clark, Jac Conaway, Keith Covington, Carol Hunt, Kim Rosen, Cynthia Schwartzberg, Brian Stokes, Mary MacGill Stokes, Donovan Thesenga and Susan Thesenga.

This book, then, is not an attempt to teach every lecture given by the Guide. Rather, it is an attempt to synthesize and re-tell what I have been taught, pulling this together with what I have learned along the way. As such, it is a concentrated guide for following the most direct path to self-knowing.

For those familiar with the Pathwork lectures, it is my hope that this book will help you frame the work you are doing, so you can better understand the greater arc of the path you are on and see how everything fits together. For people unfamiliar with Pathwork, may this book help you find a doorway in, or perhaps offer insights that help deepen your work on your chosen path of spiritual self-development.

I have woven many phrases and expressions from the spiritual recovery program Alcoholics Anonymous (AA) into this book, as they dovetail so beautifully with the Guide's words. I have also worked in insights from Kabbalah, which I studied for four years under the wise and caring tutelage of Kimberly Cahill. *Namaste*, Kimberly, to the mega-watt light in you.

My gratitude for all my teachers runs deep. Most especially, I am grateful for everyone I have ever gone through struggles with. You have all been my buddhas, or teachers, showing me where I had work to do. Thank you for walking with me on this journey homeward.

   – Jill Loree

Contents

Tapping the Source | The Lectures and Q&As

Like a map, this book is not the place itself. The primary source of wisdom is the Guide, a spirit entity who delivered volumes of wise and caring teachings in the form of lectures. References to these lectures appear throughout this book to encourage further exploration. They are placed based on relevance to topics, and do not always directly address the information presented.

These lectures were given by Eva Pierrakos, who spoke the words of the Guide, and are the foundation of the Pathwork® program for spiritual self-discovery. They are all available for free at www.pathwork.org.

You can also find many answers about life in *The Guide Speaks*. This is an arrangement, by topic, of all the answers the Guide gave to questions asked at the lectures and Q&A sessions. These can be read for free at www.theguidespeaks.com.

PART I: COMING TO LIFE

There is actually no contradiction between the idea that we are responsible for our own fate and also that powers beyond our scope must complete the creative process. Consider a gardener who must prepare the soil, but who does not make the plant grow:

- Preparing our own consciousness is like the gardener preparing the soil.
- Eliminating wrong concepts is like the gardener pulling up weeds.
- Removing our blocks is like removing rocks in the soil that hinder the spreading of the roots and later the plants.
- Implanting truthful concepts is like planting the seeds.
- Cultivating the proper attitude and patiently waiting until the seed has taken root and can sprout is like tending the soil, seeing that it has sufficient light, moisture and nourishment.

With these steps, the gardener fulfills his or her job, calling the creative process into existence, making it possible for it to take place. But it is not the gardener who possesses the ability to make a tree or a fruit or a flower out of a seed. If the gardener wants a certain plant, the proper seed must be sown, but it is not up to him or her to accomplish the growth.

There is nothing in the world the gardener can do to actually make the seed develop into the plant. Nothing. A creative process is at work that re-quires the gardener's cooperation; there are certain conditions the gardener alone can fulfill. But then nature must do its job.

We often wish for a specific result, but what we sow is the seed for the very opposite result. This causes distrust of life. Seeing how we bring forth exactly what was sown—even the negative results—must strengthen our confidence in the principle of the creative process.

Finding the Treasure | The Self

L ife is all about the journey, not the destination. Yet it's important to have a sense of where we're going. In short, this is a journey to knowing the self.

Working with the teachings offered by the Guide, we begin to understand the journey of our soul and to apply these teachings actively in our lives—not just theoretically in our minds—to make authentic, positive changes that transform us and the lives we create.

Here is an overview of the many steps and stages we will be exploring, that every human being goes through in our journey back to the Oneness, which is both our origin and our destination. In fact, being in a state of unity is our God-given birthright.

Key Aspects of the Journey

Unity

All is one.

The Fall

Used our free will to experience negative aspects of divine qualities; Caused masculine-feminine split and inner splits; Descended into dark spheres ruled by Lucifer, the first to fall.

The Plan of Salvation

Christ's plan that gives us a path for returning to God; Christ came to Earth as Jesus to unlock the door for us to escape Lucifer's dominion, if we choose.

~Incarnation~

Take on a task to heal a certain aspect of our negativity in this lifetime.

Transference

Our soul split is transferred onto our parents.

Needs Not Met

Child wants 100% perfect, exclusive love and to always have its way; Due to the nature of reality, this results in painful feelings of rejection and frustration, which make the child feel inferior.

Images

Wrong conclusions about self, others and life are generalized and go into the unconscious.

Body Blocks

Resistance to painful feelings creates frozen energetic blocks that are held in the body.

Defenses

Child chooses a strategy to avoid pain: Aggression, Submission or Withdrawal.

Mask

Lower Self demands love, turning defenses into a Power, Love or Serenity mask to get its way.

Idealized Self-Image

Mask of perfection designed to compensate for missing self-esteem and bring love.

Inner Critic
Internalized voice of parents becomes cruel to self.

Faults
Lower Self uses various distorted ways to overcome its fear of humiliation (fear) and feelings of inferiority (pride); It wants to win and won't let others off the hook (self-will).

Negative Pleasure
Pleasure current has gotten attached to painful experiences during childhood; Life force is later activated through destructiveness.

Negative Intention
Lower Self resists giving or giving in; Uses Images to justify resistance; Stays stuck and therefore stays in separation.

No-Current
Hidden faulty belief says No to fulfillment, making Yes-current frantic and ineffective.

Vicious Circles
Negative patterns are continually recreated resulting in pain, hate, shame, guilt and self-punishment.

~Purification~
Bring all this into conscious awareness; Call on God to help correct wrong thinking, release unfelt pain, re-educate the inner child, and visualize a new reality based on truth.

~Transformation~
Activate the greater consciousness within.

Unity
Continually, consciously surrender to God; Experience self as one with all.

The first stage of this work is the clearing of obstacles. The Guide calls this the purification process. As we go through life, we need to learn to slow down and recognize when we are in an emotional reaction. It is always best if we can take the responsibility to do our own work of self-knowing before we react in a way that leaves us with more to clean up.

In the 1950s, 60s and 70s, when the Guide was being channeled through Eva, encounter groups were new and people were often unskilled in how to uncover dark areas within the psyche without acting out harsh negative feelings directly towards others. A lot of re-wounding happened. Today, we know that it is possible to access these feelings without acting them out.

We do this by talking openly with a qualified person—a therapist or spiritual healer—which brings things out from hiding. Opening up to another is an act of humility, and in that moment, we do not want to appear more perfect than we are. That brings a relief our spirit has cried for, even if the person does not give us a single piece of advice. This is the same benefit people get from confession in certain religions or from what's called a "fifth step" in Alcoholics Anonymous.

The intent of this spiritual path is to work with all areas of the psyche that are negative, destructive or in error, and to activate the greater consciousness within. So it must then deal with issues that today are often also dealt with in therapy. The difference is in the intention. Therapy is typically sought to address a specific aspect of life that is not going well.

A spiritual path is a lifelong journey of self-searching in which everything becomes fodder for discovering what is hidden in the psyche. People who are struggling with active addiction, depression, borderline tendencies or similar issues should seek appropriate qualified assistance before embarking on a spiritual path such as this.

The second stage of this work is the transformation in which we continually activate the greater universal consciousness. We need to discover that there is an inexhaustible fountain of strength and inspiration within. As we can see, this cannot be done sequentially. We need to cultivate regular contact with our spiritual center as best we can from early in our journey, so that the ego learns to let go and activate the greater forces of the Higher Self.

Over time, we also need to be willing to let go of our life stories. The past is only important because it caused us to develop these unproductive ways that are responsible for our present pain. We want to go all the way through our issues to reach full resolution and avoid getting mired in recycling old wounds.

On the surface, growth and stagnation can seem similar because they both move in circles. So sometimes people believe they are in a growing process—which is a spiral—when in fact they are merely going around in circles. Undirected self-confrontation often leads to this. Where we might exaggerate one thing and underestimate another, someone detached from our problems may see things in the right light.

On the other hand, those who are truly in a growth process may feel temporarily discouraged, believing they are going around in circles. This cannot be avoided. We need to make the same recognitions on deeper and deeper levels of a spiral until we converge on the key point from which the problem can be resolved.

At that point, we may be given a test by the Spirit World. It can be very helpful to remember this to avoid falling into feelings of despair. But whenever the transition to the next circle is made, the reality of it will fill us to the depth of our being. We will then know that we are not moving in a stationary circle.

In a similar way, the Guide's teachings are a spiral, taking an important concept and deliberating on it from various different angles. One might say there are two parallel spiral movements: one pursues the disturbance, and the other shows the true picture that complements it.

There are also rhythms to the work that may look like this: breakthrough, release, relief, new hope and light, contraction, self-doubt, doubt about this path, hopelessness. Know that over time, the good periods increase in depth and duration, and the negative periods will decrease.

The rhythms of expansion, restriction and stasis are impacted by the big and little splits that occur when our misconceptions form, and that adhere to our soul substance. This may cause self-alienation—as we may essentially create a separate self as a means of protection—and to not know our own rhythm.

"Again and again you search in vain for the real you, the core of your being. You are confused because you take the superimpositions to be the real you, simply because you have become so used to them. You may have discovered their destructiveness, their artificiality, but you are as yet still unable to dispense with them. You have not yet gained the sense, awareness, and experience of the real you. You ask yourself, "Who am I? Where is my real self?"

I attempt to guide you to the core of your nature from various angles, through various approaches. I can help you, but you have to do the work of recognizing, of facing, of changing. In short, it is your struggle. If you want to become happy, to lead a fruitful, rich life, you have to be whole, undivided. And this can be only if you are your real self. It is logical and reasonable that the struggle and the effort have to be yours, if you wish to realize yourself.

The state of self-alienation — that of not being one's real self — is so predominant that its symptoms are not conspicuous. You miss noticing them because they are so general that you assume them to be 'normal'."

– Pathwork Lecture #95

In nearly every lecture, the Guide offers a promise as well as a problem or duality, a way out, and a prayer or meditation. In general, here are some of the promises of what the Guide says we can expect if we follow these teachings: we will be less depressed, tiredness will cease, we have strength to go through our difficulties, we will bear our cross in the right way, we will know what our lives are all about, we will enjoy life in spite of difficulties, and we will be vibrantly alive.

Learn more in *Finding Gold: The Search for our Own Precious Self,* which explores these teachings about self-knowing in greater depth.

"If you demand of your life—and therefore of any path you contemplate entering—to bypass feeling your anxiety and your pain, to avoid owning up to your dishonesties, your cheating, your spitefulness, your games, and your more or less subtle pretenses, then it might be better for you not to start on this path.

But if you expect a real effort and are prepared to embark on the journey into yourself to find, acknowledge and bring out whatever is in you, if you summon all your inner truthfulness and commitment for the journey, if you find the courage and humility not to appear other than you are even in your own eyes, then you have indeed every right to expect that this path will help you realize your full life, and fulfill your longing in every conceivable way. This is a realistic hope. You will increasingly know it to be so."

– Pathwork Lecture #204

Walking the Walk | Relationships

The purpose of creation is connection, or fusion, and to this end, a great irresistible force motivates us toward unification. In fact, fusion with another person happens on four levels: mental, emotional, physical and spiritual.

If we are unified and without inner conflicts, our relationship experiences will be fulfilling, joyous, nourishing and sustaining, adding creative power to the universal reservoir. But in reality, everyone has fragmented aspects that are in need of healing. So the question is: how do we overcome our conflicts to have this?

For infants, closeness is passive—babies only receive. This is as it should be. But for adults, closeness must be mutual with a giving and receiving by both partners. Too often though, our distortions create hard inner walls so that energy cannot flow; we cannot give and we cannot receive. When we're blocked, there is no fusion and no pleasure, only perpetual frustration.

On the mental thinking level, then, we must learn to express ourselves, even when this is difficult. Not doing so is dishonest and is due to fear of unpleasantness and an unwillingness to risk exposure and confrontation. In short, we won't do the hard work of going to a more profound level.

What we discover is that we can only communicate in a healthy way—

and without guilt—by eliminating our own cruelty; we must release any hidden motive to hurt the other. The energy of our inner tyrant needs to be converted to positive aggression so we can take care of ourselves and set healthy boundaries. Then, when our cruelty is gone and are we no longer stuck in blame, we can speak up.

- If we can't exchange honestly without cruelty, where is the fear in us?
- What cruelty in us makes us afraid to say what we see?
- Where is our blindness that makes us unsure, defensive and hostile?

A loving connection on the emotional level is expressed by perceiving the complexities and potential of the other. We put aside our ego needs and expectations and make ourselves empty so we can receive the expressions of our partner. Our deep, deep yearning is to really know another—to find true belonging through two people revealing themselves to each other. The Guide tells us that a lifetime would not be enough time to fully know another soul.

We also have a wish for a close physical connection that is in harmony. But if attraction on this level is only for procreation or pleasure, it will not embody this fuller connection, so it will be superficial and disappointing.

To enjoy the full wonders of a spiritual connection then, we must attend to whatever arises in our relationships, becoming willing to risk being vulnerable, and exposing and confronting whatever calls our attention. This is the doorway we must go through if we want to experience bliss. *The Pull: Relationships and their Spiritual Significance* explores this topic more deeply.

The Guide calls relationships a "path within a path." This is because our ability to be in a loving relationship depends on our ability to give and receive, which depends on our ability to perceive reality, which depends on our ability to be undefended, which depends on our ability to suffer pain and frustration free from manipulative interpretations. So to be in a relationship is to have our spiritual work laid out in front of us.

For fusion, we must give what we long to receive, including: tenderness, trust, respect, patience, and recognition of another's capacity for growth; we must offer the other the benefit of the doubt, allowing room for alternative interpretations and letting them unfold their inner essence. When we can let others be who they are, we have the freedom to be our real selves. These are all aspects of mature love.

Images are not really the cause of problems in relationship, the Lower Self is. It uses our mistaken beliefs to hold us in patterns that cause us to stay locked in negative intentionality that says, "I don't really want to give myself to this relationship."

We take self-responsibility for this when we delve into how we are the ones recreating our childhood hurts. We want to do this with a loving intention toward ourselves, and not from the inner tyrant that drives us like a slave-master toward growth. We can only dismantle old patterns bit by bit.

Self-knowledge, self-love and security are all prerequisites to love. Of course, there are degrees and it is not an either-or—we grow and develop these as we go. Sometimes we try to overcome our insecurities through outside pursuits, such as doing good deeds for society. But this often belongs under the heading of escape because security cannot be found outside the self. That doesn't mean one should cease doing good works, but it needs to accompany establishing a center of gravity within.

To the degree insecurity permeates the soul, the capacity for loving is absent. If we are insecure, we cannot trust ourselves. And if we do not trust ourselves, how can we love ourselves? And we need to love ourselves before we can love another. So healthy self-love and inner security are linked, and lead to the ability to love others, which is the highest point on the scale of loving.

Five Stages of Love

1. **Love for inanimate objects** | This is lowest on the scale. Objects do not oppose. They do not require the complicated mechanism of perceiving the feelings of another. They do not disapprove or criticize. They demand a minimum of personal sacrifice or consideration. Objects will make no demands.

2. **Love for abstract ideas, principles, art and nature, and love for one's profession** | Love for abstract ideas evades personal

involvement with the accompanying apparent risks, but at least it moves the mind, soul or spirit in some measure. It may also require some personal contact and confrontation with others of different opinions. Love for ideas and principles is certainly more outgoing than the isolating pursuit of loving mere objects.

3. Love for plants and animals | They require a certain amount of sacrifice and consideration, putting one's immediate selfish comfort aside. It does not require the risk of rejection, nor taking the trouble of pondering what the other's needs are, or the effort to establish mutual understanding. To a very minor degree this may apply to keeping and caring for an animal, but certainly not to the degree required in a close relationship with another human being, where one's senses have to be alert to the other person as well as to oneself.

4. Love for humankind as a whole | This may still relieve a person from intimate personal involvement—the most taxing form of love, and therefore the most fulfilling one. But it does require effort, thought, the willingness to sacrifice, activity, and many other attitudes that are highly constructive. This applies only if such love is followed through in practice, rather than remaining just a theory.

5. Love for individuals in close, intimate relationship | This is highest on the scale, and most constructive. The fact that we often demonstrate love through turbulent behaviors that have nothing to do with genuine love—but indicate immature needs and dependency and often bring disharmony—still furthers development and our capacity for love. A life of turbulent relationships may be infinitely less harmonious than the life of a hermit or a recluse, but the process of inner growth cannot be gauged by apparent outer harmony.

Consider where love for God would fall on this scale. Is it love for abstract ideas and principles? If so, it can be an escape. For if it is healthy and genuine, our love for God manifests through our love for others with whom we are able to communicate and relate. This, in turn, cannot happen unless we overcome our fears and vanities; unless we find and dissolve the obstructions in us that make us unable and unwilling to love.

We need to have the humility to admit the limitations of our understanding of the inconceivable and incomprehensible existence of the Creator of all beings. And then we can turn our attention to the things human beings can learn—namely, to love other human beings.

To love God as an idea does not require practical involvement and the willingness to put one's egocentric aims below the needs of another person. So it is possible that an avowed non-believer who is willing to work toward a loving connection with another person is in fact closer to loving God than a professed believer who isolates.

During the Fall, as explained in *Holy Moly: The Story of Duality, Darkness and a Daring Rescue*, our souls split in two. One aspect of this is the division into masculine and feminine halves, but it is never a perfectly clean split. This means a person will be male or female for most lifetimes, but will also experience the other gender for some lifetimes.

Our longing for union comes from this inherent knowing that another more complete way of being is possible. In some cases, we will be able to reunite with our "soul mate" in this lifetime. In other cases, for a variety of reasons—all of which are in keeping with God's laws and our karma—we may not. When that is the case, we can still be united with another whom we can love.

Both activity and passivity exist in both men and woman but we manifest different aspects. Our work over the course of many incarnations is to focus on the aspect of development that will bring us more into harmony within ourselves.

The woman's activity should enliven her receptivity, keeping her vibrant and in fluid perpetual movement. Man's active currents should bring out his passivity, preventing the active current from becoming too aggressive. By rounding and mellowing it, passivity will take the edges off and slow down the abrupt and too-quick motion of an overactive current.

The same holds true of other supposedly male and female aspects. Without the soul qualities of love, kindness and intuition that open the road to understanding, intelligence and reason will not bring constructive results. On the other hand, love, kindness and intuition, if not kindled by discrimination—which is the result of reason and intelligence—can easily be lost in wrong channels and become destructive.

Further, we need to overcome our mass image that love is weakening and dangerous. In this way, we will find the courage to love.

Keeping it Real | Time & Money

The Plan of Salvation, as described in *Holy Moly*, explains the reality that we have all come from previous hellish spheres. There, we lived in a condensed matter—much thicker than the matter on Earth. Nature was totally absent, nothing was alive, nothing had flavor. Our inner nature was also equally inaccessible. On that sphere, there is no birth and no death—this is a distortion of eternity. It is hopelessness itself and existence is totally mechanized. The principle of evil prevailing there is materialism.

In the last century, this aspect of evil has taken over Earth. The lifeline to reality has been broken, resulting in an alienating reality in which humanity has prided itself on its advanced state. We became a reality onto ourselves. The good news is that this has brought people back to taking self-responsibility for searching within, and it is not coincidental that the science of psychology has emerged. The bad news is that we have produced a life not that much different from that dark sphere we came from.

Materialism shows up on this dualistic Earth plane in the form of "having" and "not having." Of course, on the unitive plane, there is always a way out, which is this: we must learn to give. Because the Law of Giving and Receiving states that receiving is impossible when the soul withholds its innate yearning to give—one cannot exist without the other.

When we are in the illusion that we are empty and impoverished, we automatically create a vicious circle. This belief makes us hoard ourselves—

our riches and our talents. We are holding in rather than giving out, which separates us from the riches that surround and penetrate us, confirming the belief of our poverty.

In contrast, a benign circle can be created by risking giving out; we need to consciously expect that abundance will grow. As we start giving to God in trust and with love, we lift the lever that locked the mechanism. Words can never describe the magnificence of realizing that grace is all around and that the more we receive the more we can give, and the more we give the more are we capable of receiving. Then giving and receiving become one.

Learn more in *Blinded by Fear*, Chapter 1: The Mother of All Fears: Fear of Self (Subhead: Giving and Receiving)

False pictures are reinforced by our beliefs, just as true pictures are. Only when they are questioned do they lose their energy. We need to unearth and challenge our false beliefs, which is like pulling out poisonous weeds and planting new beautiful seedlings. One such obstacle is our tendency to build on deficit. It links to our belief that we live in an empty, poor, ungiving universe where only some can "have".

When we build positive beliefs and life patterns on top of hidden negative beliefs, we build on deficit. Same when we secretly believe that we are a totally unlovable and unacceptable human being. Or when our real and false guilts prevent us from turning ourselves fully over to God. When we assume the universe is hostile and we protect ourselves with destructive defenses, we build on deficit.

Building on deficit can appear to succeed for a while. That is the trouble. It is like building a house on sandy ground. It may hold up for while, but when it starts to crumble, we may have forgotten we chose to build on such a weak foundation.

This path is directly designed to create an inner order, painful as this may be at first. In this way, we can begin to build on real assets and never allow our "inner economics" to become fraudulent and unsound. All personal crises—all breakdowns—are nothing but bankruptcy exposed.

We need to stop living above our means, covering one hole with a newly created hole. This is true for individuals as well as governments. Whenever a country goes through a severe crisis—riots, wars or financial collapse—it is a result of waiting too long to establish order in a controlled way. It results from not wanting to expose the deficits so that true abundance can follow.

This step can only be possible through faith in God. Risking to have faith can create faith. A balanced, harmonious, abundant world order requires direct communication with the divine world and the Christ within and around us. If we ignore his existence, we cannot perceive his presence. Nor can we hear his guidance.

We need to connect with Christ within to summon up the courage needed to temporarily expose inner bankruptcy—which is reflected in outer bankruptcy—for both people and countries. Then we will be able to also examine when the individual needs to give more to the collective entity, and when the process can be reversed. The law will fulfill itself so that none will come to deprivation from their giving—quite the contrary, more abundance will accrue for them.

Learn more in *Pearls*, Chapter 7: Basking in Grace & Not Building on Deficit.

Many spiritual teachings talk about the need to be in the present moment—in the Now. The Guide advocates we use a Daily Review as one of the best means toward living each day and each hour fully. If we don't do this work daily, we are not fully on this path.

In time, after having recognized, in all its depth, a distortion or a negative attitude in ourselves, we will experience a special peace that is full of the spark of aliveness. That the recognition itself may be very unflattering and disillusioning about oneself, and at times even painful, will not diminish this great experience once the recognition is complete.

It is so only because, at that moment, we have fully utilized what is given to us—the fragment of time at our disposal. Too often, we are right in it, but blind to it. We merely try to get out of the Now without utilizing it.

Traditions are an example of where we may experience duality that relates to time. They come about when some great beautiful truth breaks through into our physical world, and we want to continue to experience an expression of it.

Some people may get stuck on the notion that all things from the past have value, and therefore they reject change. But change is what was needed to inspire a tradition to begin with. Others swing to the other side and say only new things have value, rejecting all traditions.

Both can be true. True traditions can be very dynamic and alive; others have become empty gestures and should be let go.

Learn more in *Pearls*, Chapter 6: Unwinding Humanity's Relationship with Time.

Crafting Our World | Words

The Bible says "In the beginning was the word," which speaks to the power of words to create—whether they are silent, spoken or written. But there are some words we have developed such a strong negative reaction to, it is like an allergy. "Evil" is one such word.

When we deny our vulnerability, our feelings of shame and being helpless, and our feeling of being unlovable, we create destructive feelings and attitudes—and that is evil. Evil is a defense against suffering. But denial of these original experiences compels us to re-experience them over and over again, and in doing so, we increase the suffering and perpetuate evil.

The Guide tells us we can more correctly interpret the Biblical phrase "resist not evil" to mean that *resistance is the evil*. Resistance is a tightening up against the flowing movement of love and truth. It is a slowed down consciousness that can only exist as resistance to good. It always obstructs some beautiful, valuable aspect of creation. In the end, resistance really is futile. Because eventually a crisis occurs, which is the breaking point between two opposite desires—evolution and resistance of truth.

"You have begun to understand that to the degree your Lower Self is conscious—thereby enabling you to choose not to act upon it and to pray for help to purify it—you are invulnerable to evil."
– Pathwork Lecture #248

Learn more in *Pearls*, Chapter 13: Uncloaking the Three Faces of Evil: Separation, Materialism and Confusion.

We resist through laziness and self-indulgence, as well as by distracting ourselves and not being honest about our emotional reactions. Then we project our distortions onto others, blaming them and not seeing how the darkness lives in us. The Guide calls that a "sin"—another loaded word.

"Jesus" is yet another such word. In his series *Resurrecting Jesus*, spiritual teacher Adyashanti suggests we reframe our sins as being the places where we "miss the mark." The Guide defines a sin as the lack of love resulting from immaturity of the soul. Immaturity means separateness, and in separateness, one does not love and is therefore "in sin."

Seven Cardinal Sins

Covetousness | Wanting to have and own what is not yours, which comes from a place of deprivation.

Lust | A selfish desire from child consciousness to receive without having to give, without a true spirit of mutuality.

Anger | A cover to real feelings such as pain, which may also move to collapse.

Gluttony | A distorted way to try to be fulfilled when real inner needs are not fulfilled.

Envy | Wanting to destroy and take what we can't have because we feel so empty.

Pride | When we did not receive "good-enough" mirroring, we did not get a clear view of a healthy self; this leads to feeling inadequate. Pride is a way to help us feel important.

Sloth | The collapse, when aggression and submission don't work, that goes to indifference and apathy.

It is important that we not let our reactions to these words keep us from receiving the deeper meaning of these teachings. For this reason, as well as the fact that words can lose their meaning after too much repetition, the Guide often uses alternative words to describe the same thing. For example, divine essence, universal power and greater consciousness are all different expressions for that one hard-to-name word: God.

"Om is another word for God. There are many languages with many different words for the ultimate Creator. It truly does not matter which language you use, provided your mind connects with the source of all that is."
– The Pathwork Guide in Q&A #244

The Guide explains that the Bible is the most unique document, holding meanings on many levels. This is true despite the mistranslations and human errors that have inevitably crept into it. It is written this way to assure that only those who are truly doing the work of self-knowing will be able to access the deeper meanings.

When people use the most fundamental meaning to support their negativity, they are unknowingly falling for one of the three principles of evil, which is confusion. This includes half-truths that subtly turn into lies without being easily traced because they are presented under the guise of divine truth and therefore seem unassailable. Such confusion is an effective weapon of evil.

During the decades of Question-and-Answer sessions, the Guide invited participants to ask questions about Bible verses so they could receive a deeper explanation of their meaning. These can be read in *Bible Me This: Releasing the Riddles of Holy Scripture,* or under the topic The Bible at www.theguidespeaks.com.

"What is the word?…Each word is a blueprint essential for building the structure…It is plan, knowledge, opinion and consciousness. The word is feeling, attitude and intentionality…The word is what is behind all creation...It can be the divine will or the will of the cut-off, ignorant and destructive particle of consciousness. Be it conscious or not, the word is the sum total of your beliefs in any given area where you speak the word. It is the sun that creates the planets. It is energizing force and it is design. So much is contained in the word."

    – Pathwork Lecture #233

Learn more in *Pearls*, Chapter 8: Articulating the Power of the Word.

Tuning It In | Balance & Order

According to the Guide, God's world is an orderly one. But unlike the way we perceive structure—which is rigid and unchanging—in the Spirit World, the more structure something has, the more fluid it is. This paradox is evident when we begin to tune into our intuition, or guidance, hoping to find a mistake-proof fence we can lean on to be safe. But if we do that, we are then actually less safe, because we are relying on illusion. In reality, life is constantly in flux.

Our ability to balance the active and passive forces is what allows us to bend with the winds of life, and yet be strong enough to hold our own. We sometimes have the erroneous belief that to be active is to use our free will, and to be passive is to align with God's will. This, the Guide says, is simply not true. We need willpower to fulfill God's will.

Willpower, which is use of our free will, is not the same as self-will, which is the will of the immature, unhealed ego. Where our will needs to learn passivity is in accepting other people and situations as they are; these are the things we cannot change.

When we push our active will into places we should be passive—accepting life on life's terms—we create congestion. And when we are passive where an action is called for, we create stagnation. This stagnation can permeate our whole being, not just one facet.

When we accept something on the surface but secretly harbor resistance, there is an inner revolt—which is active. These hidden tensions are what others feel, even when we bite our tongue. There is something the Lower Self wants—or demands—and this needs to be found.

Desire is an active force that when positive, helps us overcome our weaknesses. It pushes us to be honest—both with ourselves and others. When we lie to others, we know we are lying. But when we stay in blindness, we are really lying to ourselves—and that is far worse. This blindness is what blocks our knowing God's will.

The Serenity Prayer

> God grant me the
> Serenity to accept the things I cannot change, the
> Courage to change the things I can, and the
> Wisdom to know the difference.

Rarely do we need a transcendent revelation to know God's will—we just need to look within. In this way, we can continually, consciously surrender our will to God's will, tuning into each moment and praying for the highest good for all concerned.

We need to learn to trust God's will for us. When we do this, we will develop our connection to the greater consciousness that is infinitely reliable. But due to our own blocks and distortions, our intuition will never be a fence we can lean on.

Learn more in *Living Light*: Chapter 1: Searching the Serenity Prayer to Find God's Will: The Forces of Activity and Passivity; in *Pearls*, Chapter 11: Bringing Ourselves to Order, Inside and Out; and in *Gems*, Chapter 6: Finding Balance Within Instead of Banking on Outer Rules.

Opening the Veils | The Spirit World

This opening of our perspective about life can widen our lens, helping us feel the sidewalls of the greater container that holds us as we go through darker parts of our journey. If we lose sight of this, we can lose our way in the brambles of the Lower Self.

One thing we can and should do is actively, consciously call spirits of truth and light to us. Even if we don't do this, when we overcome a fault, or fight our Lower Self and align with our desire to fulfill the will of God, we emanate a substance that draws spirits of light toward us.

By the same token, if we give in to our Lower Self, violating divine law, we emanate a quality that draws the spirits of darkness nearer, like a magnet. Emanating anger draws spirits of anger; selfishness will draw a specialist who will encourage us further in this fault; and so on. What comes out of us is what we draw toward us. Like attracts like.

There is a mutual activity the goes on here with the spirits of darkness. It goes like this: they fulfill a task in their world of darkness when they win out over a person, particularly with someone who loves and seeks God. They are very keen on drawing us away from God.

But they are particularly keen on conquering people who seek God, trying to get them to give in to their weaknesses. The spirits earn special rewards in their world for such work. They know very well that they cannot accomplish anything by trying to inspire us to do any type of wickedness that is foreign to us. But they can succeed with the seemingly harmless faults that draw us slowly but surely further into darkness, depression, self-despising moods, and thus into separation from God.

It is not so much the fault in itself that is damaging, but rather that we become disgusted with ourselves and may thus give up the fight altogether. Stumbling into the same fault in itself is not bad, provided it is recognized and one learns from it by adopting the right and constructive attitude.

As a matter of fact, no progress is possible without stumbling. But when the stumbling is viewed with an attitude of hopelessness and self-disgust, then the clouds become bigger and bigger. Then a person gets more and more involved with the respective dark spirits, and with the world of darkness altogether.

We do not have to commit a crime in order to live in the world of darkness. There are other vibrations that can accomplish this. If, however, a person refuses to be an instrument for the powers of darkness, if we fight—and we can only do this by knowing our own faults extremely well, for only through them can we be tempted by the dark spirits—guess what happens.

The dark spirit will rise higher in its development—it will learn. Not directly, not immediately, because it is still so much in darkness that at first it will only know defeat. This defeat will cost it its position, so that it suffers, and only this suffering will bring it nearer to God. Because only then will it turn to God, as a last resort, in complete despair.

As long as it can claim victories in its world of darkness and has power there, it will never turn to God. So each victory, even the smallest one, of each human being, causes a tremendous chain reaction in the universe among beings of whom we are not even aware.

The Guide tells us that if we could know how much we accomplish by our victory—for ourselves and for so many other spirits as well—we would really try much harder. And not only evil spirits are affected by our victories, but also erring spirits who do not belong anywhere. They are often around us and learn from our victories in a much more direct way than those dark spirits.

So when we conquer ourselves, we are in fact a vital part of the great Plan of Salvation. We are then an active soldier in the fight. We are a front line soldier. And a front line soldier needs better weapons, more strength, and better protection than one who does not fight back or one who is in the hinterland. The weapons and the strength come to us from the Spirit World of God in guidance, enlightenment and recognition.

"Never forget that we are always there with you, no matter how close the dark spirits are allowed to come to you at certain times. We watch over you and see to it that they can never overstep their line. The last word is always you!

Do you permit yourself to know where your thoughts and decisions come from? Do you wish to listen to these voices, or perhaps to turn to the voice that is at times more removed and harder to discern?

At such times you need to assert your will to remain with God and serve him even stronger. You need to question the easiest way that comes to you. When you do this, you will always triumph, as God must finally triumph over Satan. The light of Christ is the strongest there is, and with it, you must be safe."

– The Pathwork Guide in Q&A #247

On a bigger arc, our journey moves from experiencing ourselves as a child of our parents, to understanding the bigger holding—we are a child of God. To set the stage for this journey, the Guide's earliest lectures were about creating a framework for understanding the Spirit World. More can be read under the topic Spirit World at www.theguidespeaks.com.

"Question: You say we should be in contact with the Spirit World of God, and that other spirits will harm us spiritually and even physically. But isn't everything God's world?

The Guide: It is like this: there is God's great Creation with its wonderful laws, and it includes all the spirits he has also created and to whom he has given free will. A great number of these spirits have voluntarily accepted God's laws and his order and have thus remained happy. A great number of other spirits have broken that order, again voluntarily, and by that act they have created unhappiness and disharmony for themselves.

For happiness can lie only in the wisdom of God's laws. All spirits who have at one time or another broken this law and have not yet found their way back to recognize this law as the only wisdom, the only right course, stand outside this order – voluntarily – just as they could voluntarily accept it. And one day they will. But as long as this does not happen by their own volition and conviction, they will remain outside the world of God.

God does not force any creature; choice has to come from the free will of each individual. Ultimately, and such is the beauty and perfection of God's laws, every single child of God will return – return to the enlightenment and wisdom, to the happiness and freedom that can be found only in divine law.

There are almost as many human beings as spirits who fall into one or the other of these two categories: those belonging to the divine order and those outside of it. The former are perhaps helping, working, cooperating in the great Plan of Salvation. The entities in this group, among other things, find out in spiritual endeavor where they are still unconsciously deviating from the laws. And then there are those, many of them, who do not accept God's laws, who create chaos in their surroundings and in their own selves, by wanting to follow their own very incomplete laws."

– Pathwork Lecture #11

Turning the Corner | A New Age

M ankind evolves gradually, alternating between phases focused on individuals and then groups, individuals-groups, individuals-groups. We cultivate our own resources and then come together, communicate and interact. This overlays on the spiral movements we each experience when we do our own work.

We must work out our negativity individually as well as collectively, for the collective soul is the sum total of the individuals. Working in both ways is tremendously necessary.

The Aquarian Age brings us closer to overcoming our duality of "me versus the other." The work we do in groups is a different facet from working by ourselves, allowing us to reveal ourselves and be accepted, which can challenge deeply held misconceptions.

Every smallest group can be truthful together and develop real feelings of affection. The value of this is tremendous, rippling out an unpretentious way of being that has a great influence on a universal scale. Individually, it helps a person overcome shame and separateness, so that real living can begin. This is what has arrived with the dawning of the new age at the turn of the century—the Age of Aquarius.

Learn more in *After the Ego: Insights from the Pathwork® Guide on How to Wake Up,* and *Blinded by Fear: Insights From the Pathwork® Guide* on *How to Face Our Fears*; and in *Gems*, Chapter 3: How Consciousness Evolves Between Individuals and Groups.

Leading the Way | Jesus Christ

There are three main ways we can learn from Jesus Christ. The first is to follow his teachings as taught in the Bible; many explanations of Jesus' teachings are provided in *Bible Me This*. The second is to look to his life as a teaching. For example, in working with the Stations of the Cross, we can experience how the steps on our personal journey mirror the final path of Jesus Christ*.

Jesus is Betrayed | We all have experiences of being hurt by others and situations in life. We are disillusioned, realizing that the utopia we fantasized will never be. Life is impermanent, loss is inevitable, and others are fallible.

Jesus is Condemned to Die | Every childhood holds experiences that feel like life or death. Our egos struggle to reign supreme; we come to realize the limits of our humanity and fully accept the state of our development at this point.

Jesus Carries his Cross | We begin the journey of purification compassionately and honestly accepting and facing our Lower Self, and challenging the truth of our images. We stumble along the way, but each failure and "beautiful problem" becomes a steppingstone for growing on our path. We give up the idea that anyone else is going to do it for us, and we embrace a deeper sense of self-responsibility. As the deeper negative intention to stay separate is met and humility deepens, we see that others can help us to carry our burdens, if we let them.

Jesus is Nailed to the Cross | We become stripped bare of our defenses and we surrender to our vulnerability. We fully and finally experience the pain of our separation from God, from ourselves and from others. We become willing to wake up to the truth about our illusions.

Jesus is Resurrected | There is a period of waiting between death and rebirth. We patiently allow God's will to guide us, staying in not knowing—without expectation—until we awaken and a new awareness is born in us.

*From *Resurrecting Jesus within the Pathwork: Footsteps on the Path to Waking Up,* led by Jill Loree and Beth Hedquist at Pathwork Members' Weekend & Jamboree, Sevenoaks Retreat Center, August 2014.

Looking more closely at the step of betrayal, the Guide teaches that betrayal is impacted by an image that affects everyone—a mass image—due to our blend of imperfection and desire for perfection. We each have a demand to be special and have others agree with us in order to make our inferiority feeling vanish. This goes deeper than pride.

The duality is: rebel against what others think or say versus pleading for admiration. We often do both at the same time. The truth is that we can't please the whole world and be true to ourselves and our life plan.

When we are betrayed, we are hurt and disappointed, even though we were loyal. The offender, however, claims to have been betrayed by us, accusing us of doing the same thing that caused us pain. We are most hurt by being accused of being disloyal or dishonest.

The truth is that no mishap occurs that we have not caused in some way. Our unconscious beliefs are stronger than the conscious ones, so they drive what manifests. Our part may be hard to detect because our actions were correct. The hidden piece is that we desire an elevated position in the world's eyes, to convince ourselves that our inferiority feelings are unjustified—or we will die.

The truth is that our emotional survival depends only on our own opinion of ourselves. The more we cater to the opinions of others, the less we think of ourselves. This is a vicious circle. The way out involves uncovering our hidden desire for specialness, and then being willing to "hang on our cross," feeling the pain of letting this go.

Learn more in *Living Light*, Chapter 18: THE MASS IMAGE OF SELF-IMPORTANCE | The Folly of Needing to Feel Special.

The third way, which is by far the most important, is to learn the greater story about why Jesus came here to Earth. For starters, it is important to recognize that we are made of the same stuff as Jesus—it is called the Christ, or Christ consciousness.

"The truth is, my friends, whether we want to believe it now or not, that Jesus, the man, was the incarnation of the Christ. And this spirit is the highest and most exalted of all created beings.

He is the first direct and inborn creation of God. His substance is the same as the substance of God. All of we possess some of this substance, which I call the Higher Self or the divine spark. It has to come out gradually through spiritual development.

But no other created being has this substance in quite the same degree as the Christ. And there is the difference."

– Pathwork Lecture #19

As with the word "Jesus," we often react strongly to the word "salvation." In short, it just means that the door to heaven is open to us, and we can make the choice to walk through.

"Salvation means, among other things, Christ's endless forgiveness and acceptance. It means that we can always find your way to God, no matter what we have done, and no matter what your Lower Self still wishes to do. The door is always open, we are never, never locked out.

All we have to do is knock. Ask for the bread of God's mercy, love, forgiveness and personal help in all ways, and we shall not receive a stone."

– Pathwork Lecture #258

If we think of our sins as being the ways we have missed the mark, then perhaps we see that it is going to be our job to right our wrongs. There are three paradoxical aspects to this:

1. Only we ourselves can effect our salvation. It is our responsibility.
2. We cannot possibly do it alone. We need the help of others who share the journey with us, who may often see what we do not see.
3. Without God—without the personal assistance of the personal aspect of God—the undertaking is too vast for us to accomplish.

So this is our work, and we need help to do it. But no one, including Jesus Christ, can or should do this for us.

"My friends, if you study all the Scriptures from this point of view, you will get an entirely different understanding of them. I am quite sure that the reason for the life and death of Christ will now make sense to you.

There would not be any sense in Christ dying on the cross for sins others have committed. If you have committed a sin, you yourself have to straighten it out and no one else can or should do it for you. If someone else were to do it for you, you would not gain purification. You would not receive the strength through the process of self-purification, which alone will protect you from committing sins again.

As long as the evil root is not torn out, it must again produce impure fruit. Only you can tear out the roots of your evil. Therefore, that was not the reason Christ suffered and died."

– Pathwork Lecture #22

In the story of the Fall, the Guide explains how we, through our free will, made the choice to experience the negative aspect of divine qualities. During the ensuing Fall, our souls split, and this split is what we transfer onto our parents so that we can see it and thereby heal it.

"This is the way Christ has opened the door. You may now understand why it is said that Christ saved you from your sins. This is accurate only in the sense that your great sin of falling, of not remaining faithful to God, and of becoming at one time part of the world of darkness does not have as a consequence eternal exclusion from the divine worlds.

From this Christ has indeed saved you, and for this you certainly have all the reason in the world to be grateful to him. Through him you now have the possibility by your own efforts and development to cross the threshold.

In that sense, it is correct to say that Christ died for your sins. However, the interpretation that Christ died for all your sins and all your faults is very wrong."

– Pathwork Lecture #22

This story, as told more fully in *Holy Moly: The Story of Duality, Darkness and a Daring Rescue*, reveals how the journey of our souls has taken us into the realm of Lucifer, from which we now desire to leave. Until we make the decision for God though, we will be held under Lucifer's dominion, returning to spheres of darkness when we sleep and when we die.

Opening to the reality of Christ and this work of transformation is the key to opening the door that leads to heaven. We've all been through hell already. The question is, for how long are we willing to keep going back?

"The light I bring is always the light of Christ. He has said he is the truth and he is the way and he is life. In his light you find the way to truth in the smallest and largest issues, in personal and impersonal issues.

This way leads to the love of the Creator who has given eternal life. Eternal life can be found only in truth. The way to the truth leads through the mazes of the dark areas in our own soul; through encountering the temptation to remain in them and savor their passing gratification; through the deliberate overcoming of this temptation.

The great Christ light is the overpowering love of the Creator, of creation, of all that is. Be blessed. Choose this way."

    – Pathwork Lecture #248

In walking this path, there is nothing we must believe. But because Jesus is the Christ and this way leads to truth, eventually we must come to know this truth, and to therefore believe. It cannot be any other way than this. And so we can see that many Christian religions have taught truths mixed with some misunderstanding. They simply haven't been holding the whole truth.

Making the Loop | Reincarnation

When we have no awareness of self, there is harmony. When we begin to have limited awareness that there are pieces of ourselves we don't know, we sense the disharmony. When we reach full awareness, we will be in harmony again.

When we incarnated into this lifetime, it was with the intention to heal some aspect of ourselves—some disharmony—so we can find our way back home to God. So life, which always operates according to God's divine laws, gives us the lessons we need for that to happen. The friction and disharmony we experience on Earth—bumping up against other souls who have their own imperfections—gives us exactly what we need to heal and grow.

The journey of the soul can only be understood by realizing that we incarnate many, many times before we are fully healed and reunited with God. It is not possible for anyone to do it another way.

God's laws are infinite and just. There is good reason for everything that happens. The anesthesia we experience when we incarnate is an example of this. The fact that we cannot recall previous lifetimes is with good reason, and we should not spend effort trying to unearth them.

If knowledge of a previous lifetime would be helpful for us, it will come to us through our intuitive channel. If this happens, it will feel like the sacred gift

39

that it is, and we won't want to share it with just anyone. If anything, the Guide suggests we think about what our next lifetime or two will be about—what is the work we have yet to do?

It is possible that if we complete our task for this lifetime, reincarnation can happen within the same lifespan. The Guide was clear that this is something a person needs to sense for themselves. No outer entity will be able to validate this for us if we feel this may be part of our journey.

What may be more important to recognize is any belief we harbor that doing this work and completing our task will cause us to die. Death is always something a soul agrees to on another level. The reasons for a shortened lifetime are many and cannot be generalized. More can be read under the topics Death and Reincarnation at www.theguidespeaks.com.

In all cases, our own main inner split will be transferred onto our parents. This split will hold opposites, with each parent activating one aspect of the split. For example, if the split is "it is painful to be seen and it is painful not to be seen," one parent will act aggressively toward the child, making it painful to be seen, and the other will not be able to see the child, which will be painful. Both parents are of course acting from their own blindness. The attempt to do two opposite things at once—be seen and not be seen—creates tremendous tension and turmoil in the soul.

All reaction to authority is a projection of one's soul split onto another person. When triggered into a trance, we are in transference and not seeing the other clearly for who they are. Transference is also an important aspect of the healing journey, which a trained Helper or healer will be aware of and will hold with the care and attention needed for doing this sensitive work.

Since everyone arrives on this planet by way of the Fall, it becomes clear why everyone experiences pain and frustration during childhood. In our immaturity, we tend to blame our parents for our pain.

But if we back up a step, we see that we are on a far bigger journey. We are coming from a place of darkness—that was caused by our own choices. The experiences in our childhood are actually an effect of causes we set in motion. So what initially appears as a cause—that our parents created our pain and suffering—can be seen from a greater perspective of truth to be an effect. Suddenly the world doesn't seem so random.

Learn more in *Bones*, Chapter 11: Our Habit of Transferring our Split onto Everyone.

If we are parents, this work may reveal to us the ways in which we have fallen short. No good will come from using this as a weapon towards the self. We can express the pain of realizing that in our blindness we have hurt another. But our job as parents is not to save our children from the work they have come here to do. They too have a Higher Self, spirit guides and a task.

While parents have the most influence in a child's life, others including teachers, siblings or anyone closely related, also can make impressions in the child's malleable soul substance. By doing this work, we can model a more authentic way of living and create a container in which the child can learn. When we overreact, we can own our mistakes. We can learn to tune in to what is really needed in each situation, instead of relying on rules.

We can give the gift of being present, creating a space for our children to grow and make mistakes. In this way, we can help them surface faulty beliefs before they get buried deeper, and make it safe for them to feel all their feelings. Creating security for our children can move mountains.

Learn more in *Pearls*, Chapter 5: Preparing for Reincarnation: Every Life Counts.

We know that if we go to the gym and stand next to a weight machine, our body will not become stronger. To build physical strength, we need to have something to push against. So it is with our soul. In the Spirit World, like attracts like, and we hang out with other spirits who are at a similar level of development. While more comfortable perhaps, this doesn't motivate us to heal or grow.

In the Spirit World, the word for our planet, "Earth," basically translates to "land of lack of awareness." Earth is a sphere inhabited by a great range of souls who are all blind in some way and who differ in their level of development. By bumping up against others who have their own blindness, our issues come to the surface. This is how we grow. We can become bitter, or we can become better.

It is not an accident that we cannot know another's level of spiritual development just by looking at them, and there is nothing gained from judging where another is on their journey. The only thing that matters is our willingness to look within ourselves. But we can be sure that if we are reading these words, more is expected of us than being a decent person.

When starting down a spiritual path to self-knowing, it may be tempting to want to bring everyone along. Trust that each person has his or her own inner plan, and lead by example. Then if others notice our light and want what we have, they will ask. It's all about attraction, not promotion.

The more we evolve along our path, the more important it becomes that we continue to do our own work, clearing away every little speck of blindness that appears. Because the bigger a person's light, the bigger the shadow it can cast if even the tiniest distortion gets swept under a rug.

We evolve slowly from one incarnation to the next. As we do, we rediscover the Higher-Self quality of humility hidden beneath our Lower-Self pride and feelings of inferiority. Self-confidence will naturally develop. We will have gratitude not only for the support we receive—for it is only with the support of God and our guides in the Spirit World that we can heal and grow—but also for the challenges that act as fertilizer for good growth and healing. Then being "more evolved" or "more enlightened" will not become an ego trip. It would be like asking: which is better, an adult or a child?

Learn more in *Living Light*, Chapter 3: SELF-CONFIDENCE | How Can We Get More?

Creation is shaped in such a marvelous way that whatever distortions exist, in the process of working them out and transforming them back into their original way, even the distortion itself can become useful to the entire process of evolution.

So, for example, the drug problem of the 1960s and 1970s was an expression of souls with certain misplaced needs that were being fulfilled in a destructive way. The Spirit World made very positive use of the distortion. The taking of drugs opened spiritual doors for a great number of souls who would otherwise have remained totally dead to all inner levels of reality.

This does not mean that taking drugs is recommended, for there is surely a much better way to open these doors. However, as long as the conditions existed in these souls as they were, a large influx of spiritual reality—no matter how it was gained—came into a very materialistic world full of very separated consciousness.

PART II: MEETING THE SELVES

People are complicated. There are many layers of the self, and various aspects tend to overlap and borrow traits from one another. This makes it difficult to explore this material in a linear fashion. Here is a brief introduction to the layers, each of which will be explored in greater depth.

The Higher Self

The Higher Self takes practice to connect with, it may not have words, and it is full of paradox. It is all things that are good and serve connection with the self, others and all that is. It says, "I can't do this alone" and surrenders to God.

The Lower Self

The Guide teaches that any truth can be distorted, and that's really what the Lower Self is—a distortion of pleasure into pain. All negativity derives from the cross-over of pleasure and pain. Because Lower Self contains pleasure, we cannot get rid of it until we find the pleasure in the destruction. Then we can reconvert that distorted energy back into its loving, flowing form. To do this, we must also understand and correct the associated wrong thinking.

The Little-L Lower Self

Little-L Lower Self is the ignorant, illogical inner child who wants 100% perfect, exclusive love and to always have its way. Neither are possible so it feels rejected and frustrated. Not having these false needs met makes the child feel inferior, so it draws wrong conclusions about its value. It develops other faulty ideas about itself, others and life.

It suffers from being trapped in life-or-death duality, and from feeling scared and rejected. It attempts to block these painful feelings by stopping its breath, thereby freezing the energy of these feelings in the body. Its response to life is "I can't," as in "I can't feel this, or I'll die."

It attaches its natural drive for pleasure—which is its life force—to the painful experiences. To avoid future pain, it chooses a defense, but this doesn't work. It dons a mask of perfection designed to compensate for the missing self-esteem, hoping that if it is perfect enough, it will get love. This also doesn't work.

The Big-L Lower Self

Big-L Lower Self creeps in, turning the child's defense into a strategy to win. It wants to rule. It demands love but resists giving. Its intention is to stay stuck and stay separate, not letting the parents off the hook for the pain they caused.

This hidden tyrant is cruel to the self through inner criticism, and to others through bullying, betraying, holding back and seducing/rejecting. It derives pleasure from this destruction, activating the life force by recreating the painful climate of the child. It uses the misconceptions of the child to justify all of this.

The Lower Self uses competitiveness to overcome feelings of inferiority, building cases against others and maligning them. It fears the pain of humiliation and sets a negative intention to never give in. Its response to life is "I won't," as in "I won't give and I won't ever give in."

The Mask

When we begin down this path, shame is the first thing we run into. It is the feeling we are exposing something we need to hide, and is the outer layer of our mask. The mask is a strategy intended to get love and defend against pain. It does neither, and being only a strategy, it isn't real.

It uses sickly sweetness or attacks to manipulate and control others, or detaches in false serenity. It uses blame, victimhood and judgment to turn the focus outside the self. The Idealized Self-Image attempts to create a perfect version of the self, but it is fake and instead creates more rejection.

The Ego

The unhealed ego is immature and wants to reign supreme, saying, "See me, I'm better than you, love me for it." It uses drugs and distractions to avoid focusing, and to escape or transcend itself. It needs to become strong enough to make a choice to seek God. It is a necessary servant for the soul to do this work, but it is not the master.

The mature adult ego is the compassionate, objective observer that chooses to connect the Higher Self with the inner child. It prays to see the truth, surrenders, and needs to die many little deaths. It will eventually dissolve into the Higher Self. The healthy ego commits, wants to see misconceptions, and is willing to pay the price.

The Universal Self

While it is essential to dissolve childhood conflicts, the greater aim of this work is to transition from the isolated, self-centered, dualistic state to the state of union with all that is. Our objective must not stop short at the purification of the Lower Self but strive endlessly toward this greater fulfillment in the unitive state of consciousness.

The Story of Two Wolves | Native American Indian Wisdom

An old Cherokee is teaching his grandson about life. "A fight is going on inside me," he said to the boy. "It is a terrible fight and it is between two wolves. One is evil—he is anger, envy, sorrow, regret, greed, arrogance, self-pity, guilt, resentment, inferiority, lies, false pride, superiority and ego."

He continued, "The other is good—he is joy, peace, love, hope, serenity, humility, kindness, benevolence, empathy, generosity, truth, compassion and faith. The same fight is going on inside you—and inside every other person, too."

The grandson thought about it for a minute and then asked his grandfather, "Which wolf will win?" The old Cherokee simply replied, "The one you feed."

Learn more in *Bones*, Chapter 3: The Higher Self, the Lower Self, and the Mask Self.

Digging for Gold | The Higher Self

E very human is a divine being at their center. Words tend to fail us in
trying to describe this Godself inside us. Other expressions that mean
the same thing include: the Oneness, universal consciousness, divine spark,
core essence, higher power, Holy Ghost, and Christ consciousness, to name
but a few. The main catchall phrase used in these teachings is Higher Self.
Whatever we call it, the truth is that everyone is, at their core, all good, and
we're all of God.

But often we look around and it doesn't really seem that way. We encounter other people who are self-centered and unkind. Some days, we face
conflict at every turn. Without a doubt, life on Earth with our fellow inhab-
itants can sometimes seem downright cruel. Say again, where exactly is God
to be found in all of this? In fact, on this path of spiritual growth and healing,
we learn that the light of God is often hidden behind layers of darkness.
Some spiritual teachings call this the shadow; the Guide calls it our Lower
Self.

So while our light may shine through in certain areas of our lives, it is
covered over in others. Our work then is to uncover whatever is blocking us
from living from our Higher Self in any and all areas of our lives. When we
do this, we will uncover our already-existing connection with all that is; we
will experience the peace that surpasses all understanding; we will know that
all is well.

On a spiritual journey, there is a shift from believing God is outside one-self, to realizing God is within. For some, this journey may involve pulling away from organized religion—where one goes to a special place, such as a church, to connect with God. Others may end up hanging out in an atheistic or agnostic place of believing there must be no God, or simply not knowing what to believe.

But because this longing to know God is really coming from within, it never completely goes away. Whether we know it or not, every single being on this planet is seeking to know God.

The teachings from the Guide are all leading us to discover this truth of the divine within and to live fully from this inner core, or real self. To do that, we must discover who we truly are, and that takes a bit of work.

This journey of self-finding is not in opposition to any faith or religion. If we are getting nourishment and fulfillment in any of the world's faith tra-ditions, the Guide encourages that we continue—even as we may open to new thoughts from these teachings.

All well-known faiths and religions have something of value to offer. And all also have distortions. We are humans—it cannot be otherwise. It has been the same with the community created around these teachings from the Guide.

In the end, this work of self-discovery boils down to coming to know our-selves. Because if we do that, we come to know God. There is nothing we must believe to do this. Along the way we will grapple with doubt, without which we would indeed be gullible. But on this path, we need to become willing to doubt even our doubts.

Learn more in *Gems*, Chapter 12: Four Pragmatic Steps for Finding Faith and Addressing Doubt.

If we could hear God's words being spoken lovingly to each one of us, it would sound like this:

> I am working through you.
> I am in all your thoughts, if you wish to hear me.
> I am in all you see, if you wish to see me.
> I am in all the words you speak,
>   if you wish me to express through you.
> I am in all your actions, if that be your commitment.
>
> And as I manifest through you,
>   you rediscover life in new terms.
> You will see that life is a glorious Oneness
>   in which there is nothing to fear.
> What need you fear if you discover me?
> What need you fear if you identify with me?
>
> Know that you are God.
> As such you can never die.
> Give that which is you now—in your thinking,
>   in your being, in your perceptions—to me.
> As you give yourself to me, so must you be eternal.

– Pathwork Lecture #236

This Higher Self of ours—this inner Godself—has never been negatively affected by anything that has happened. It is an aspect of our being that never comes and never goes—it just is. So then, if we don't feel close to God, who moved?

The three major divine attributes of our Higher Self are wisdom, courage and love. This explains the enduring popularity of the movie, *The Wizard of Oz*, where brains, courage and heart are the tickets home. We each have one of these qualities as our primary essence, but all three are always present in each person, and when they are in balance they complement one another.

Our Higher Self is our conscience—that part of us that, deep down, knows we should be decent, love others, have faith and be kind. It is made of the finest, most radiant light and vibrates at the quickest frequency. The voice of the Higher Self is soft-spoken, so we must listen intently to hear its calling.

Higher-Self qualities include compassion, acceptance, humility, patience, understanding, honesty, authenticity, generosity, humor, perceptiveness and kindness. Our goal is to uncover and strengthen these attributes in ourselves.

So then embarking on a spiritual path such as this is like putting on Dorothy's ruby slippers and discovering that everything we need is already within us and we can always find our way home—if we are willing to follow a path to self-knowing.

Many spiritual disciplines teach the truth that there is only one force in the universe, which is love. Love then is at the core of who we are. So when we have any negative emotions, we are not in alignment with the center of our own being. Pain is what arises from the tensions created by our own obstructions to our Higher Self, and from our struggle to avoid them. But friends, facing our Lower Self is exactly what we came here to do.

Earth is a plane of duality, so it holds both pleasure and pain, making it a match for the current condition of our soul: we are capable of pleasure but we're also holding onto pain. To love in this realm, then—to access the core of ourselves—means we must become willing to feel both pleasure and pain: said another way, we must be willing to feel pain and keep our hearts open anyways.

So stepping into awareness of who we are—of living from our loving core—requires that we feel the pain we cause ourselves; this is the most important step to healing. Our ego needs to die many little deaths in coming to terms with our self-generated pain, until we realize that feeling this pain will not kill us. Then and only then will we be living in reality.

The Higher Self, by contrast, exists on the unitive plane of consciousness, so it can hold the opposites of duality but is not trapped in duality. So the

Higher Self, we discover, sits comfortably with paradox.

This means that when we get trapped in the illusion of duality—when we see things as good versus bad, right versus wrong, white versus black—we are trapped by the Lower Self. We don't want to look at this, so we focus our attention on someone or something outside ourselves and we project our wounds onto them; we see our dualistic splits "out there."

What we need to start doing is turn around and look inward, to uncover the unfortunate misunderstandings and the immature demands of our Lower Self, along with our perpetual self-evasion. To do this, we need to get in touch with our own fear. Because when we are afraid to fully see ourselves, we stay in blindness.

We could describe the process of enlightenment as continuous, conscious surrender to this process of self-discovery and being in self-awareness. But let's be clear, it is unrealistic to hope that we can reach enlightenment—to live our lives from the Oneness within—without going through the hard work of unearthing whatever is blocking our light.

Everyone has areas of blindness. We miss the whole point of living though when we hope to stay in the dark, believing we can avoid looking at ourselves forever. In doing this work of self-discovery, it helps immensely to have compassion and acceptance for the inevitable blind spots we discover in ourselves and others. And we need to remember that whenever we see an aspect of the Lower Self, it is always the Higher Self that is holding the light.

"Lord, help me to forgive those who sin differently than I do."
– *Crucial Conversations: Tools for Talking When Stakes are High,* Kerry Patterson and Others

Learn more in *Gems*, Chapter 8: The Pain of Injustice and the Truth about Fairness.

It is a spiritual law that we cannot skip steps. If we do, we shall stumble and make this work harder than it already is. Plus, we will just have to back up and fill in the missing steps. It is also a spiritual law that there is always a price to pay, and we have to become willing to pay it. Spiritual bypassing refers to the desire to skip steps and not pay the price of doing this work.

This can happen when one wants to be more "evolved" than one really is, especially after having made some good initial progress. This is pride and it needs to be addressed. In its essence, humility is a Higher Self quality that we can develop by continually accepting and then purifying whatever negativity may arise in any moment.

A humble person is not concerned with how evolved others perceive him or her to be. What matters is finding one's core, and following the will of God. This is why this path is not about overlaying any beliefs, mantras, affirmations, altered states or positive thinking over buried faulty ideas. Because in the long run, such shortcuts do not work.

"What is to give light must endure burning."
– Victor Frankl

Seeing the Mirror | The Unconscious

J ust as we need to rotate our internal mirrors to catch the reflections of our Higher Self, we need to become accustomed to looking for other less desirable hidden parts of ourselves. For example, we each harbor misconceptions about life that we are not even aware of. Our main misconception is "what we don't know doesn't exist and therefore won't hurt us."

Denial is a key defense we use to avoid trouble, but it leads to nothing but more trouble. It acts by stagnating our energy so that feelings cannot move. As a result, one of the best ways to surface what's lurking in our unconscious is to look around and see what's bothering us. Where are we stuck?

If there is any disharmony in our life that is causing an "emotional reaction" in us, that is our key that there is something in us that needs to be addressed. Emotional reactions are responses we have to people or life events that are bigger than the situation would seem to warrant. In short, we're triggered. We need to learn to bring reason to our emotions and discover the real root cause of our reactions.

Unlike a normal emotional response, these don't move through with a natural peak and release. Emotional reactions get stuck in us, because we have actually bumped up against a stuck, or frozen, place within ourselves. Whatever it is, we can't let it go—it seems to have a hold on us.

Our first immature reaction is to blame something or someone outside ourselves for having caused our reaction. This gives the other person all our power. We then feel we have no boundaries because we are powerless; this is how we make ourselves a victim.

What we don't want to look at is the way in which this troubling thing lives inside of us. That, in fact, is the last thing we want to consider. We believe that if the offending person or situation would stop or go away, we would be OK.

But that's not the way life works. In fact, it's just the opposite. This thing has actually shown up in our life because it has been magnetically attracted to us due to the very reality that somehow, in some way, it lives in us. This is where the work begins.

"This path demands from an individual that which most people are least willing to give: truthfulness with the self, exposure of what exists now, elimination of masks and pretenses, and the experience of one's naked vulnerability."
– Pathwork Lecture #204

This distortion inside us is a twisted stream of energy and consciousness that has gotten frozen in our bodies and in our beings. What was once a positive force has somehow gotten blocked and distorted into a negative force. If we can't see this negativity in ourselves, our focus will go onto something outside ourselves, and we will see it there. Hence the saying, "You spot it, you got it."

If we choose to turn away from looking at it, what we will find is that much to our dismay, unpleasant situations will turn up again and again and again. It may look slightly different each time, but eventually we can begin to realize there is a pattern.

To gain more clarity and insight into the root of the problem, the Guide encourages us to spend a few minutes at the end of each day doing a Daily Review. We simply jot down a few words about where we felt disharmony during the day, and what our primary feelings or reactions were. Over time, these patterns will begin to reveal themselves to us.

It is true that wherever we go, there we are—complete with these inner distortions that keep attracting people and circumstances designed to help surface the inner distortion for deep growth and healing. This is the loving plan of God's laws—that all negativity will bring about results that will motivate us eventually to turn and look at the real origin of the distortion, inside ourselves.

We need to find the courage to see our hidden places. And usually, we can't see them without someone holding a mirror up to us. Such a person is not really our enemy; they are a teacher helping us see our own selves.

Disconnection is painful. In fact, nothing is more frightening and tormenting than feeling the effect of a cause we ourselves have set in motion but do not understand. It is through our commitment to working with whatever arises in life that we come to see how cause and effect are linked, and in this way we begin to take on a new level of self-responsibility. Gradually, that's what turns the tide.

In the end, truth is love and love is truth. So in areas of our life that are working well, we have already resolved inner misunderstandings and our Higher Self is shining brightly—we are in truth and love is able to flow. Such positive benign circles will continue forever because that is where we are already in truth.

Where our light is blocked, that is the place to turn our attention—without losing sight of the fact that this dark area is not all of us. But this is where we are still separated from God and our own Higher Self qualities; this is where we are not yet in truth.

Ignoring these areas will not help them heal, nor will they just go away. In fact, the longer such areas are ignored or pushed aside, the greater the likelihood that a major crisis or chaos will erupt in our life. This is not the result of an uncaring universe or a punishing God. Rather, it is a natural effect of a cause we have set in motion by continually turning away from what calls for our attention, and which needs to be healed inside us.

"The personality must see eventually that all eruptions, breakdowns, crises, mean to tear down the old structure so as to re-erect a new and better functioning one. The 'dark night' of the mystics is such a time of the break-down of old structures...

Crisis can be avoided by looking at the inner truth when the first inklings of disturbance and negativity manifest on the surface. But a tremendous amount of honesty is required to challenge one's tightly cherished convictions...

If difficulties, upheavals, and pain in the individual's life, as well as in the life of humanity as a whole, were viewed from this point of view, the real meaning of crisis would be understood and much pain could be avoided. I say to you now: Do not wait for crisis to come in an eruption as the natural, balance-establishing event that takes place as inexorably as a thunderstorm must take place when certain atmospheric conditions have to be altered and clarity in the atmosphere is to be re-established.

This is exactly what happens within the human consciousness. Growth is indeed possible without intense painful 'dark nights,' if honesty with the self becomes predominant in the personality. True inner looking and deep concern with the inner being as well as giving up pet attitudes and ideas must be cultivated."

– Pathwork Lecture #183

Learn more in *Pearls*, Chapter 15: What's the Real Spiritual Meaning of Crisis?

Understanding the Child | The Little-L Lower Self

There can be a misunderstanding about what it means for an adult to be childlike versus childish. Being childlike is beautiful, and no adult can be truly joyful and creative unless we preserve and nurture our ability to be childlike. It includes the capacity to feel excitement about new things, to be adventurous, and to question and learn about new things.

To be childish, on the other hand, is to be immature. It is the inability to accept frustration or to take discipline. It is the false notion that if we do not get what we want immediately, we will perish or never be happy again.

Immaturity originates from the fact that every child wants to receive exclusive love, without limits. This is understandable but unrealistic. Further, every child wants to have their own way. This is equally unworkable. So in every child's life, there will be pain and frustration.

Worse yet, because we live on a dualistic plane filled with life-or-death thinking, the child equates pain with death. To avoid death, the child acts to stop this pain. The most effective way to do this is through control of the breath. Children literally freeze their feelings by stopping the flow of the life force—called *chi*, *ki* or *prana* in other languages—through stopping the breath.

This explains why, as adults, when we feel painful feelings arise, we will often feel a lump in our throat from reengaging those constricting muscles, and find ourselves holding our breath. It is our habitual way of cutting off the experience of pain, frustration, sadness, disappointment—whatever uncomfortable feelings we don't want to feel. But we are actually investing our life force in cutting off our own life force.

As a child, when this cutting off happened, our life force became frozen and stuck. Movement was stopped dead in its tracks. And it will remain so until we do this work of "re-membering" these frozen or split off aspects, and allowing them to become re-enlivened and reunited with the whole of our being. This means that we must now experience the pain we could not tolerate when we were children. For it is a spiritual law that life cannot be cheated, meaning in the end, we can't avoid feeling anything that is in us.

It is important to understand that before we were born, while we were still in the Spirit World, we made a choice regarding what we wanted to heal in this lifetime. In order for any of us to see our work, or task, it is necessary then that it manifest in this lifetime. So the perfect conditions have been chosen—including parents, siblings and environment—for our unique "soul dent" to come to the surface so we can see it and heal it.

When we were children, we had no adult ego available inside us to make choices about how to handle life situations. There were no higher-level-reasoning faculties to make sense of things. As adults, this has changed. Our ego now has an important role to play: it opens the gateway to our Higher Self. This makes greater resources available for supporting us in feeling and releasing these wounds.

The Gateway Prayer

Through the gateway of feeling your weakness lies your strength;
Through the gateway of feeling your pain lies your pleasure and joy;
Through the gateway of feeling your fear lies your security and safety;
Through the gateway of feeling your loneliness
   lies your capacity to have fulfillment, love and companionship;
Through the gateway of feeling your hate lies your capacity to love;
Through the gateway of feeling your hopelessness
   lies true and justified hope;

Through the gateway of accepting the lacks of your childhood
 lies your fulfillment now.

– Pathwork Lecture #190

If these painful experiences hadn't happened—but they did—and if we hadn't innocently stopped the flow of feelings so as not to feel them—but we did—we would not have these immature places in us—but we do. These are the places that get activated when something happens in life that cause us to have an emotional reaction.

In that moment, our unconscious inner child feels threatened by something that has a similar look-and-feel to a childhood experience. This child consciousness is now facing what it believes to be a life-or-death situation, and is feeling re-traumatized. As soon as this happens, we are effectively in a trance. Whatever or whoever is in front of us is now melded with the situation or person—most often a parent—from our childhood.

We may experience confusion, disassociation from our body, regression in how old we feel, and tunnel vision. We are not in our adult reasoning brain, and we don't realize that we now have the resources of our own adult ego available to us. It is the healthy, conscious adult ego that can make new choices, including opening to the Higher Self and asking for help. This adult ego needs to wake up.

Learn more in *After the Ego: Insights from the Pathwork® Guide on How to Wake Up*.

We can think of this inner child as the "Little-L Lower Self," because although it is part of what keeps us in separation, there is an "I can't" quality to it. It feels helpless to make another choice. From this place, we defend ourselves believing we need to protect ourselves from death. We are essentially saying, "I can't feel this, or I'll die."

When we have an emotional reaction and slip into a trance, we need to learn to pause, breathe, and find the part of ourselves that believes it is still in a life-or-death battle. We need to see that "that was then and this is now," teasing apart the reality of the current situation from the way it overlays something from an earlier time. It will feel like two slides have come to-gether, one on top of the other, with the two images feeling so similar it will be hard to slide them apart.

It may seem that the child's main problem is the desire for perfect love. But in truth, even if the child had received perfect love, this would not have resolved the child's problems since they are due to pre-existing beliefs from previous lives. What's more, although the child would have been satisfied with mature love—love that is imperfect and takes the risk of being hurt—the capacity to give mature love is rare, and even if one parent gives it, the other probably doesn't.

Instead of mature love, the child received distorted love, which children can feel. This creates resentment, which leads to rebellion. The three types of distorted love from parents are:

1. Parent overindulges or overcompensates as apology for not loving maturely.
2. Parent won't punish or exert healthy authority.
3. Parent is too severe or strict, bullying the child.

Unlike eternal values, which are about love, truth, wisdom and courage, temporary values are dictated by the needs of a society. So over the centu-ries, the values of a society can shift. In the past, children were treated with restriction and severity; parents' pent up hostility was acted out in this way. Today, the pendulum has swung to the other side, and the value is permis-siveness, indulgence and lack of discipline. The underlying hostility is still felt though.

It is not uncommon for such pendulum swings to occur as part of spir-itual development until the more truthful middle way is found. But if one extreme is wrong, its opposite will be just as in error. If the parents overin-dulge to atone for their irritation or impatience in parenting, they create guilt and confusion for themselves. Later the child will seek to duplicate the pleasure of the overindulgence, but since other people don't carry this guilt, they don't respond with pampering and the person ends up feeling hurt by this.

Here, the underlying desire to recreate pleasurable childhood experiences is a sign of greed and a lack of self-responsibility. It belies the desire to remain a child, and this creates shame for an adult due to unconscious anger and frustration.

The truth about parenting is that we need to follow our insides to follow eternal values. Sometimes leniency is OK and sometimes punishment is called for. There are no rules.

Receiving any kind of distorted love instead of real affection makes the child feel guilty and uncomfortable, which the child pushes into the unconscious. As adults then, we may love your parents, but we still have this unconscious resentment, which prevents forgiveness and letting go. In truth, our parents weren't perfect, but they don't need to be rejected now because of this.

If all this remains in the unconscious, we will try to fix this as an adult by unconsciously recreating the childhood hurt hoping that this time it will be different and we will win—or in other words, get the mature love we now demand. Unfortunately, this is not feasible.

The result is that we will choose a love partner who has the aspects of the parent who fell short, as well as the one who came closer to meeting our needs. We will then blindly try to force them to give us mature love. But love can't come that way. As an adult, only by giving up our childish demand will we be able to give mature love, and open the door to creating mature love with our partner.

These vicious circles we create are entirely destructive. It is an illusion we were ever defeated, therefore it is an illusion we can now win. It is also an illusion that lack of love was the tragedy we unconsciously believed it to be. The real tragedy is this recreation and our attempt to master it.

To dissolve this conflict, we must find the link between our unfulfilled childhood longings and our present problems. First, we must find the aspects of our current relationships that are like the parent we resent or despise—the one for whom we had little or no love.

Then we must re-experience the longing and hurt of the crying inner child. Realize that we may have been both happy and unhappy as a child. Know that the pain hurts more when we push it out of sight. Think of this as turning the child's pain into a healthy growing pain. We may have to work to find and feel this pain.

1. Take a current problem.
2. Strip out rationalizations that "it's them."
3. Find the next layer of emotion: anger, resentment, anxiety, frustration.
4. Feel the hurt of not being loved, which is underneath—it is the same hurt as the childhood pain.

Doing this will release our parents, and we will start to seek love by giving it rather than by expecting it. Notice too how we may have completely given up on receiving love, which is a wrong extreme.

In truth, we attract people to us with a similar immaturity or capacity to love as our parents, and then we unconsciously provoke a reaction in them that is similar. As we mature, we may bring out more maturity in the other.

We must learn to balance emotional maturity—the capacity and willing-ness to love—with intellectual maturity, which can be used to re-educate child consciousness. We need to develop both.

As we re-educate the inner child, it may be helpful to impress the point that this pain we faced as children was not really going to kill us. The idea that our defenses saved our lives only works to further terrorize this inner child who believes it was in mortal danger from painful feelings. This doesn't deny the reality that children sometimes die.

"The most frequent way of attempting to remedy the situation is in your choice of love partners. Unconsciously you will know how to choose in the partner aspects of the parent who has particularly fallen short in affection and love that is real and genuine. But you also seek in your partner aspects of the other parent who has come closer to meeting your demands.

Important as it is to find both parents represented in your partners, it is even more important and more difficult to find those aspects which represent the parent who has particularly disappointed and hurt you, the one more resented or despised and for whom you had little or no love. So you seek the parents again—in a subtle way that is not always easy to detect—in your marital partners, in your friendships, or in other human relationships.

In your subconscious, the following reactions take place: since the child in you cannot let go of the past, cannot come to terms with it, cannot forgive, cannot understand and accept, this very child in you always creates similar conditions, trying to win out in the end in order to finally master the situation instead of succumbing to it.

Losing out means being crushed—this must be avoided at all costs. The costs are high indeed, for the entire strategy is unfeasible. What the child in you sets out to accomplish cannot ever come to realization...

You have no idea how preoccupied your subconscious is with the process of reenacting the play, so to speak, only hoping that "this time it will be different." And it never is! As time goes on, each disappointment weighs heavier and your soul becomes more and more discouraged."

– Pathwork Lecture #73

Learn more in *Bones*, Chapter 8: How and Why we Recreate Childhood Hurts.

We have a clue we are in child consciousness, or an emotional reaction, when we hear ourselves using the words "always" and "never," as in "such-and-such always happens to me," or "I never get so-and-so." Then the adult ego can connect with the Higher Self and ask the question, "What is the truth of this matter?" Just asking this question brings in a more mature perspective, and the answers will open the door to re-educating this young aspect.

We do this work to integrate all the inner children who have split off at each wounding. It can be helpful to sit in meditation and sense their presence, noticing their number as well as how far away some of them have gone. It requires patience and the creation of a new safe container for them to be willing to trust this adult ego and return for healing. As such, this work of healing is a soul retrieval that reunites and integrates the shattered soul.

Some people's memories from childhood have sunken so far out of their awareness they can no longer connect with them. The Guide tells us we need not worry about this, because everything we need to know is playing itself out right now in our daily lives.

This is a result of the magnetic pull of these unhealed places inside us, drawing life experiences to us that will allow us to see what is really going on inside. We can't heal what we can't see, and we came here to heal.

What heals the wound is the divine love and energy that fills up the space where the wound was, once it has been felt and released. We actively pray for this healing and then become receptive to receiving divine energy.

"When we have no territory to defend, God rushes in to where God always was. This is a paradox we understand only as we embrace life fully."
– *The Instruction Manual for Receiving God,* by Jason Shulman

Embracing the Whole | Duality vs Unity

Let's take a closer look at this dualistic way of thinking, because if we understand it, we have a better chance of not becoming caught in it. Duality is the condition of opposites wherein white comes with black, good comes with bad, and yes, pleasure comes with pain. But of course duality is not the whole game; *that* would be unity. We came from the Oneness, we are part of the Oneness, and we are heading back to the Oneness. But for now, we are stuck here in the Twoness.

We stumble into duality when we find ourselves caught in some trap with two equally unappealing options, a "damned if you do, damned if you don't" conundrum. Here, opposites are identical only in their ugliness. An example might be when we find ourselves stuck in a bad relationship: if I stay, I will be lonely and feel worthless; if I go, I will be alone and feel worthless.

We get snagged up in such illusions because they dovetail into a hidden, incorrect belief that's become buried in our unconscious, like "I don't matter." It's our own wrong thinking that leads us down dead-end roads in life.

So just know this: when we are caught in an either/or duality, we are not in truth. The only way out is to pray to know the greater truth, because prayer is the way for the split-off ego to contact the unified self—our divine center filled with infinite wisdom, love and courage.

But in that moment, it will seem like the hardest thing to ask "What is the truth of the matter?" The duality-drenched ego has gotten locked in a life-or-death struggle to be right—where being wrong feels like death—and it can't find a way out.

"This time," we think, "I can win." But we can't, because we keep on attracting people and situations that match our hidden wrong conclusions. If we pray deeply, however, greater truth will surface. Knock and the door will always open. It is when we become more intent on the truth than on being right that we begin to transcend duality.

"We can't solve problems by using the same kind of thinking we used when we created them."
– Albert Einstein

From here, going deeper into the next layer of duality, we'll find that both unsatisfactory choices actually lead to one half of a bigger duality. For example, "I only matter when I'm in a relationship. I feel worthless when I am alone." It is our striving toward the "good half" with an equally strong desire to flee the "bad half" that locks us further into a no-win situation. Because the good half isn't in truth, it's just what we're facing as we're running from the bad. There's no escape on this level.

So now we are truly at the doorstep of death, and our work must be to finally learn to die. In a multitude of little ways, every day, we need to die by letting go of whatever we hope will save us from pain. We must die into feeling we don't matter, if that's our deep-down belief. Only then can we surface and claim the truth: "I matter, whether I am with someone or alone."

The thing about living in this land of duality is that whenever we strive for a certain desired goal, it brings with it, at least to some degree, an undesired one. Because black comes with white, dark comes with light, and pain comes with pleasure. Yet on the unitive plane, neither side is thinkable without the other.

This is where that "all is one" notion of unity comes in. But it's not life *or* death, it's life *and* death. Indeed, if we want the Oneness, we have to be willing to experience all sides of it. And that means rolling with the inherent pains of life.

All our defenses and coping mechanisms have roots in the dualistic notion that pain must be avoided at all costs—*or we'll just die*. We only want pleasure and we'll fight like the devil to not feel our hurts, freezing ourselves into stuckness.

The truth is, feeling pain won't kill us. What's more, when we release painful feelings, we open up. Our frozen hearts melt allowing us to feel and flow again—so we can experience pleasure, creativity and peace. This is the doorway that leads to a life of freedom, connection and joy. Truth be known, it doesn't actually hurt more to heal our pain than to hide it, and it's by stepping through the doors of duality that we find love.

A duality gets created when the child does not receive mature love. And note, given our current state of development and the way parents are chosen for each incarnation, very few children receive mature love. This is an important "set up" to understand. It is a main plot point in the script we have each, on another level of reality, agreed to.

Further, in the universal duality created by the child's demand for *exclusive* love, the child can't win. The child will be unconsciously jealous of siblings and both parents, feeling rejected and excluded. The duality is that the child wants the exclusive love of the parents, but the child suffers more if the parents don't love each other or the siblings. This "not winning" reinforces to the child that it is not loved.

The resulting opposing but equally painful thoughts might be: "This is the way it is supposed to be" versus "This is my lot in life and it is like no one else's." This will lead the child to draw negative conclusions about the self and/or life. Yet neither statement is in truth.

The truth is that parents can love more than one person, albeit imperfectly. The reality is that the child doesn't know why it feels unloved and unhappy, or the child may believe it is happy because it got *some* love. Either way, painful feelings of being unloved and unlovable will get cut off—because the child believes it will die from feeling this pain—and trapped inside. All this must be surfaced and explored.

This is where we must begin to do the hard work of dying. Every day, we can find places in us where we are hoping to avoid a buried pain We die to this illusion by going through our painful feelings and discovering that this doesn't kill us. We must also die to our immature demands to have our way *right now*, and to clinging to anything or anyone we believe has the power to save us. The ego must learn to "let go and let God," and in doing so, discover a far vaster resource of wisdom and strength.

Often, in our frustration, we will turn towards the very thing we fear, embracing the negative and resigning ourselves to feelings of hopelessness. In this case, we will often choose a substitute for satisfaction, such as material possessions or even overzealous religious convictions, which we then cling to in hopes they will bring us the happiness we long for.

If we can keep our hearts open and feel all our feelings—including the uncomfortable ones—what we discover is that we feel better after we release the cramped, rigid holding of painful feelings. We are softened and opened up by a "good cry." In this way, we get a glimpse of how pain and pleasure are one.

It is the same with giving and receiving. They are a pair that cannot be separated. So if we say we are good at giving but not receiving, we deceive ourselves. We cannot really give freely if we are not able to receive. And if we are stuck in negative intention and won't give, we cannot receive the best life has to offer.

Truth is a spectrum. And until we see the whole spectrum of truth regarding anything, we may see something as being true when we in fact don't have the full truth. We can liken our window on truth to the experience of looking out one side of a train. Through that window, we see a certain landscape. But it is quite possible that if we look out the window on the other side of the train, we will see something completely different. And yet it's all connected.

So in dualistic thinking, the world is divided into black and white. Reality, on the other hand, combines a bit of both: Sometimes they're going to like us, and sometimes they're not. For the mature adult, this is not the end of the world. And on the unitive plane, we discover that we are both right and wrong, just like everyone else. What's more, even opposites can both be right.

"The opposite of a fact is a falsehood, but the opposite of one profound truth may very well be another profound truth."
– Niels Bohr

Until we know the greater truth of any matter, we need to remain curious and be willing to widen our perspective. When something doesn't land well in us, it is because we have not yet discovered the whole truth of the matter. When that happens, energy is released and we will feel enlivened and settled by the truth. To accept that life, with all its challenges, can also be meaningful and beautiful, requires courage. Maturity results from this ability to hold such a greater level of awareness.

Stages of Development

Immature Inner Child
- Caught in duality
- Images create Emotional Reactions
- Lives in a trance
  - Automatic reflex
  - Vicious Circles
  - Either/Or situations with No Way Out

Dissolves into Mature Adult
- Healthy ego accesses Higher Self to heal inner child
- Healthy ego asks for God's guidance
- Both/And connections with others

Dissolves into Unitive Consciousness
- Higher Self, or Christ consciousness
- Plugged into guidance and intuition
- Fully in body and in harmony: energized, awake, peaceful
- Present in the Now
- Trusts
- Realizes God is me

Immaturity	Maturity
You are not in reality. • You are in a trance, or illusion.	You are in reality. • Life is not always pleasant.
Life is black & white.	There are many shades of grey.
Drama; Rigidity; Rules • You want a wall you can lean on.	Flexible; In the moment; In truth. • It's OK to not know, as this leads to knowing.
Demand slavish submission. • You want complete surrender.	You are autonomous; The other has autonomy.
The other is the center of our world. • The other must worship you.	You are the center of your world.
The child in you rules. • Wants to reign supreme.	You can like & respect others, even if they don't do your will.
Use a forcing current to get love and approval.	Sometimes they like you, and sometimes they don't.
You are not in reality, so you can never trust yourself or others.	You have reliable perception. • You trust in others with discrimination. • You trust yourself.
Weak submissiveness is a sham of love. • This sham is what you fear.	You experience many shades of love.
You refuse to love. • You won't be controlled.	Intuition functions; You are creative.
You become a submissive slave. • You fear defeat, rejection.	There is no danger; You are not enslaved.

Learn more in *Gems*, Chapter 14: How to Visualize Living in a State of Unity, and Chapter 15: Surrendering to the Double-Sided Nature of Duality.

Taming the Beast | The Big-L Lower Self

A t some point in this work, we will find the place in ourselves that really doesn't want to change—that doesn't want to give up negativity. This is the Big-L Lower Self. It is made up of frozen, blocked and distorted energy, so it vibrates at a lower frequency than Higher Self energy, and it's holding onto a great big No to life.

In this part of ourselves, we actually sort of like our faults. Further, the Lower Self has the capacity to inflict cruelty on ourselves and others: "I'll hurt you and I'll hurt me." This cruelty is the main reason we try to escape ourselves. We need to find the pleasure in our destructiveness if we hope to tame this beast.

In retaliation for having our desire for 100% perfect love rejected, our Lower Self now demands love. But it refuses to give anything, digging in its heels and saying, "I won't," or more specifically, "I won't give and I won't ever give in." This is the underlying basis of our Lower Self's negative intention to stay stuck.

Further, our Lower Self intends to have its way without paying any price for it. We might call this "self-will run riot." Plus we refuse to let our parents off the hook for the pain they caused and the humiliation that went with it. This fear of humiliation underpins many of the fears of our Lower Self.

To cap things off, we compensate for our hidden feelings of inferiority by attempting to prove we are better than others; we face the world in a spirit of competitiveness. Then we build cases against others, gossiping and maligning them in an effort to take them down. All of this is pride.

Through the combination of these three main faults of self-will, fear and pride—all other faults cascade from these three—the Lower Self always serves separation instead of connection; separation, in fact, is the Lower Self's signature move. And because it is a trickster, our Lower Self manages to hide its childish attempts at defending against further pain behind a mask—a Power Mask, a Love Mask or a Serenity Mask—all of which are ineffective strategies certain to sabotage any chance for real connection. In this way, our Lower Self hires our mask to do its dirty work.

In addition to holding back, the Lower Self will also betray others or hurt them by seducing and rejecting them. When the resulting vicious circles lead to more pain and nonfulfillment, the Lower Self will judge others in an effort to avoid feeling affected. This traps us in feeling like we're a victim, causing us to circle back and shore up our mask.

Early down the path to self-knowing, we need to become willing to take off our mask because our mask is not real; it's just a strategy for avoiding "death"—or in other words, pain—and for hiding ourselves. Our fear is that without our mask, this Lower Self is what others will see. Worse yet, we fear that this is who we really are.

First, we need to remember that behind the Lower Self is our Higher Self yearning to shine freely. Second, it is important to learn how to expose these dark aspects without acting them out. That said, when we see these darker places in others, we often find it easier to connect with them and accept them than when we are only allowed to see their mask. The Lower Self may be unpleasant, but at least it is real.

One of the most common pitfalls that happens when we start doing this work of self-discovery is we begin to see with much greater clarity the many ways in which we fall short. And then we turn the flashlight we have been holding into a club and start to attack ourselves with it. We need to watch for this and to call a halt to it when we see it. It doesn't help, and it makes following a difficult path even more challenging.

The source of this voice is the inner critic. It is a perpetual little tyrant that continually and silently beats us up, and now intends to make us stop exploring. We know that it comes from the Lower Self because it serves to keep us separate from our own self. Until we slow down and get quiet, we may have no idea what kind of cruel things this unkind internalized voice has been saying to us.

Here is how the inner critic gets created. When the child did not receive the perfect love it craved, conclusions were drawn such as "I can't be loved as I am," "They'll never love me," or "I can't succeed." These conclusions are unique to each person, and at the same time, they are all the same. They basically say, "I'm worthless, I don't matter, I'm not enough," making the child feel inferior. This creates deep resentment for which a fear of punishment builds up.

At about the age of six, a child can project into the future. The child begins to anticipate the parents, and based on these wrong conclusions, chooses a defense intended to save it from ever being hurt again.

As the child grows, this defensive behavior becomes a habit, and the conclusions that drive it sink into the unconscious. From there, these wrong conclusions have the power to create, and they create nothing but problems.

At about the age of seven, the Big-L Lower Self creeps in and starts attacking—or punishing—the self. It is the internalized voice of a parent, and it uses the wrong conclusions of the child to justify itself: "You're worthless, who do you think you are," or "They'll never love you, why do you keep trying," or "You're a loser, you'll never succeed." The specifics will vary for each person, but the harsh tone will be the same.

This inner critic—or really, inner tyrant or tormentor—is a perpetrator of cruelty to the self and it needs to be unmasked. When we won't see it inside us, we will turn it on others and become a bully. Or we will attract bullies to us, and we will see it there. Where there is a victim, there is always also a victimizer.

Don't underestimate the Lower Self. As brilliant and amazing as our Higher Self is, that's how "good" our Lower Self is. It is a crafty, convincing and sabotaging trickster that is highly creative and highly charged.

As a negative creator, it will undermine our good intentions, cleverly setting others up to behave in a way that confirms our negative beliefs. For example, the Lower Self might take the idea "I'm inferior" and use it to undermine our ability to express ourselves clearly. When we realize we're being inarticulate or babbling, we actually feel inferior, confirming our belief. We may then turn around and judge the one we're talking to as being uncaring because they lost interest in what we were saying. The Lower Self may then lash out, to "get them back", perhaps by ignoring them or sulking. But we set the whole thing up due to our misunderstanding that we're somehow inferior.

What we need to realize is that these hidden parts of ourselves are immature, but that doesn't make us bad. Often, in our childlike enthusiasm, we trip over these undeveloped aspects that don't yet know how to pace themselves, causing us to stop our flow in life, fabricate stories and manufacture walls. To unwind all of this, we need to get to know ourselves better, and that includes getting to know our own Lower Self.

We know that whatever we fight against gets stronger, so we want to dismantle the Lower Self slowly, step by step. It cannot be transformed by harshly judging it, or by judging ourselves for being caught in its tentacles. In doing that, we get further tangled in its web and the knots get tighter.

Instead, we need to expose the script the Lower Self is following. Awareness and acceptance are what's needed here for healing. Once we see the damage we are doing to ourselves, we can wake up from the trance and snap out of it.

Running for Cover | Masks & Defenses

O ur primary essence of courage, love or wisdom determines our Personality Type, which will correspondingly be a Will, Emotion or Reason Type. Be careful to not mistakenly conclude that only Reason Types are smart, only Will Types have willpower, or only Emotion Types have feelings. Everyone contains the essence of all three divine qualities, but we each lead with one.

Personality Type	Will	Emotion	Reason
Primary Essence	Courage	Love	Wisdom
Defense	Aggression	Submission	Withdrawal
Mask	Power	Love	Serenity
Main Fault	Self-Will	Fear	Pride

When we're children and we get our feelings get hurt, we first attempt to block the pain by stopping our breath. Next, a conclusion will be made that will lead to the defense that aligns with the Personality Type.

Will Types will conclude, "I don't need love," and use aggression to overtly control and push away the other. Emotion Types will conclude, "If I submit, I'll be safe," and use submission to covertly manipulate the other.

The Reason Type will conclude, "I don't matter," and use withdrawal to escape the other.

What began as a defense of the inner child is taken over by the Big-L Lower Self that incorporates these defenses into a mask that demands love. The Will Type will use a Power Mask and attacks to get its way, the Emotion Type will use a Love Mask and become sickly sweet, and the Reason Type will use a Serenity Mask, detaching and rising above it all.

Learn more in *Bones*, Chapter 4: Three Basic Personality Types: Reason, Will and Emotion, and Chapter 7: Love, Power and Serenity in Divinity or in Distortion.

The Guide calls our defenses "pseudo-solutions," because they don't actually work. Human beings are well designed to respond in the event of an actual threat. Adrenaline kicks in and we have an instinctive reaction that narrows our attention and focuses on survival. The problem here is that emotional pain is not a real threat. Feelings will not kill us.

So if the threat of pain is an illusion, the defenses created to fight this threat are equally unreal. Our defenses and masks are made up of nothing more than ineffective strategies that only succeed in further separating us from our real self.

Worse yet, the perpetual defending against an illusory enemy activates our physical system to continually produce a fight-or-flight response. Over time, the elevated cortisol level in our bodies is actually harmful. If we remain in such an activated state, we are then less able to respond in a real life-threatening event.

The bottom line is, when we are defended behind our mask, we are not in truth. So nothing can be solved by "trying harder" to improve our mask. In the end, when it comes to navigating life, strategy never works.

"If I had asked people what they wanted, they would have said faster horses."

– Henry Ford

The mask is the outer layer of our being, and it uses blame, victimhood and judgment to deflect everything away from the self while crying a false pain that says, "Don't do this to me, life!" The real pain is our blindness that keeps us alienated from our own self.

The Guide sometimes refers to the mask as a "superimposed conscience." This is because the trickster Lower Self takes a Higher Self quality and distorts it, incorporating it into the mask. So it may have a quality of "goodness" or "rightness," but it also always has a quality of fakeness.

Creation of a Mask

1. Child experiences pain.
2. Child makes a decision to avoid feeling that pain. For example, "I won't need. I won't get my needs met anyway."
3. Child fears it is unacceptable, unlovable: "I need to not have needs."
4. Child creates a mask to appear lovable.
5. Mask shows phoniness.
6. Mask brings the rejection originally feared.
7. Child feels more unacceptable.

The Way Out

1. Accept ourselves as we are.
2. Release the fear of not being loved.
3. Let Higher Self qualities come through.
4. Let people be attracted to our essence.

Before looking at masks and defenses in greater detail, consider what the reason is for learning to understand ourselves from this perspective. The goal here is to increase awareness. We cannot change something in ourselves unless we see it. So we need to learn how our psyche defends itself. In this way, we begin to take responsibility for how we show up in the world, and how we unknowingly contribute to the problems we face.

In general, we each tend to align primarily with one of the three defenses. However, we may use one type of defense in certain situations and another in others. When we realize—unconsciously, of course—that our mask isn't working, we may try changing strategies: "If being aggressive doesn't work, I'll try sucking up." Withdrawing is typically a last resort, after trying the other defenses unsuccessfully.

It can be easiest to recognize one's Personality Type by looking at what mask, or defense, is used most. Being overly identified with one's mask, however, will make it harder to give it up, and therefore harder to give up the false ideas it hides. It will also keep us from finding the real divinity that is being hidden.

For example, in its essence, true serenity is the ability to be truly objective because we do not avoid experience and emotion. We are not so involved in ourselves. Healthy power is the power to master ourselves and difficulties without proving anything to anyone. When we gain mastery, we do so for the sake of growing, not for the sake of proving our superiority.

In its essence, love is not a means to an end. In genuine, not-self-centered love, we will communicate love and understanding in healthy interdependence. Love will not take the place of missing self-respect. Following are the ways in which these divine qualities get distorted into a mask and used as a defense:*

Power Mask | Aggression Defense

Will Types have Courage as their primary essence. In distortion, Will Types use Aggression to overtly control others. They cover this up with an attacking Power Mask.

Rules | Never show vulnerability, dependence, helplessness, emotions • Always have a "fighting spirit" • Be aggressive, be strong, be independent • Don't need, be tough.

Traits | Proud of achievements • Will is the master • God-like perfection • Invulnerable, self-sufficient.

Faults | Excessive demands, hostility • Need to triumph • Jealousy • Possessiveness • Domineering • Selfishness

Takes Pride In | Lack of warmth • Never failing • Achievement • Toughness • Aggression • Ambition • Not being helpless, gullible or dependent.

Childhood Pain | Not being seen, heard or understood.

Belief | I don't need love.

Underneath | Helpless Child

Needs to die to feelings of | Helplessness

Love Mask | Submission Defense

Emotion Types have Love as their primary essence. In distortion, Emotion types use Submission to covertly control others. They cover this up with a sickly sweet Love mask.

Rules | Never assert or find fault • Love all • Comply • Sell soul to get sympathy, help, love.

Traits | Helplessness • "Modesty" • "Compassion" • "Understanding" • "Sacrifice" • "Forgiveness" • "Brotherhood"

Faults | Acquisitiveness • Greed • Appeasement • Compliance • Craving • Compulsivity

Takes Pride In | Not asserting • Being helpless • Failure • Weakness • Understanding • Modesty • Sacrifice

Childhood Pain | Not getting protective love.

Belief | If I submit, I'll be loved, protected and safe.

Underneath | Deprived Child

Needs to die to feelings of | Rage

Serenity Mask | Withdrawal Defense

Reason Types have Wisdom as their primary essence. In distortion, Reason Types use Withdrawal to avoid others. They cover this up with a detached, above-it-all Serenity Mask.

Rules | Always look benign, detached • Never be affected • Always be objective, independent • Never commit • See both sides • Remain aloof.

Traits | Looks down on emotions • Reason is the answer, must understand • Reaction to defeat is denial • Ashamed of being affected, needing love, involvement, commitment.

Faults | Avarice • Rigidity • Prejudice • Preconceived ideas • Egocentric

Takes Pride In | Not being affected • Being detached • Being objective, responsible and independent.

Childhood Pain | Not being loved • Feeling rejected, hurt, disappointed and conflicted.

Belief | I don't matter.

Underneath | Lonely child

Needs to die to feelings of | Pain

Personality-Types Chart: Love, Power and Serenity as Distortions; Moira Shaw,1992.

At our deepest—or highest—level, we really are all connected. Or as they say, all is one. So when we hurt ourselves, we hurt others, and vice versa. As such, we do harm to others—just as we harm ourselves—when we are in our mask. Because withholding robs us of our feelings, submission robs us of independence and strength, and aggression pushes people away and openly hurts them with false superiority.

The pains, rejections, frustrations and disappointments we are working so hard to cover up and avoid seem incredibly personal to each of us. But they are really experiences shared by everyone. In fact, we have each come here to Earth to transform certain negative traits. In this way, we really are one. See if you can feel the dignity of this instead of getting bogged down in hopelessness at their discovery.

The version of our mask referred to as our Idealized Self-Image is intended to supply our missing self-confidence by showing the world an idealized version of ourselves. This, we think, is what will bring us peace of mind and pleasure supreme. It is characterized by shoulds and excuses, and unfortunately always leads to frustration.

We have a clue we are in our mask when we have an inner feeling of urgency. We can be on the lookout for statements from the mask that may start with "I must always…" and "I must never…" For example, "I must always figure everything out by my myself. I must never look stupid." When our mask fails us—i.e., we think we look stupid in a situation—the feeling can be described as glass breaking inside. Ironically, until we bring this into our conscious awareness, we will resort to the unsuccessful tactics of the mask to avoid this feeling.

The moment we can identify that we are being defended and in our mask, our observer self, or mature ego, is now not trapped in it. In that moment, we can begin to pray to see the truth of the matter: "I don't have all the answers. I can take a risk and be vulnerable. If I make a mistake, this will not kill me."

Then we die to this truth, releasing the pain and fear that has gotten trapped in with the false demands of the mask. When we do this, the tension held in the body is released and our heart softens. The Guide tells us our prayers for truth will never be answered with a stone. Knock and the door will be opened.

Learn more in *Bones*, Chapter 6: The Origin and Outcome of the Idealized Self-Image.

Deep in our psyche we know that a more perfect existence is possible— but not here on planet Earth. We harbor a hidden belief that if we can become perfect—or at least pretend that we are perfect—we will get what we want.

But isn't it actually true that we feel much closer to someone who is willing to be vulnerable and undefended, letting us see their humanity? It is one of the ironies of life that we approach perfection the more we are honest and in truth about the fallible beings we are.

Learn more in *Pearls*, Chapter 9: Why Flubbing on Perfection is the Way to Find Joy.

Letting It Go | The Ego

On the level of the human personality, it is clear we are not all of one mind. Truth is, we're divided even within ourselves. And this fragmentation is the reason we are here. The mission for each of us is to heal our destructive tendencies and bring ourselves into harmony by becoming whole again.

As long as we remain fractured and discombobulated, we are in a state of inner chaos and the mobile won't hang straight. But to have a chance at restoring ourselves to balance, we need a way to keep all our bits from flying apart. Enter the human ego, which acts like strings for our proverbial life-mobile.

The ego itself is a fragmented aspect of the whole, but it's been given a specific job: reunite the various split off aspects and then blend in. In fact, the ego is essentially made up of the same basic energy and consciousness as that substance with which it will ultimately reunite: the real self.

The real self can be equated with the essential nature of life and all of creation. It experiences fully, knows deeply, feels completely and creates beautifully. Everything wise and life-expanding comes from the real, true self. Sounds wonderful. So why don't we just live from there?

Because our true self has gotten covered over by the distortions of our Lower Self. Getting through the walls and wily ways of the Lower Self requires that we take action using our outer will—which is the part of ourselves we have direct access to—and this is under the control of the ego. We don't have direct access to our true self.

To illustrate, we can liken our ego to our hands and feet, and our true self to our heart and blood. We can control the movement of a hand or foot, but not our heartbeat or circulation. To affect our circulation, we can exercise our bodies, but we don't have direct access to affecting the flow of our blood. In a similar way, we cannot directly change our emotions, but we can determine the direction of our thinking, which ultimately can change undesirable feelings. This is the way we must go.

Unfortunately, we too often attempt to use our outer will, or ego, in ways that don't work, so we gradually weaken our ego and wear ourselves out. This happens, for example, when we over-think things or worry, believing that this "effort" will affect a situation over which we actually have no direct control. Rather than letting go and letting the true self lead, the ego grasps at straws.

After a while, the weak, sick ego often wants to give itself up simply because it cannot bear itself any longer. Now the ego will attempt to relax or let go using means that are really just escapes, like drugs and alcohol. More extreme forms of releasing an over-functioning ego are insanity, and less extreme forms include "checking out" and being disconnected from life.

Remember, we're really only here to reunite our unhinged parts. So what now?

Letting go from a base of strength is the way to achieve that one thing we all deeply long for: happiness. This is also the way to tap our inner intelligence and wisdom, which is by far greater than our directly available ego-mind. To properly let go then, we need to begin with a healthy, balanced ego.

To start, let's consider some of the roles of the ego. It is the part of us that thinks, acts, decides, memorizes, learns, repeats, copies, remembers, sorts out, selects, and moves inward or outward. In short, the ego is really good at taking things in, straightening them up and spitting them back out. What the ego can't do is add deep meaning to life or produce creative solutions, as it has no profound wisdom of its own.

"All really beautiful, valid, constructive, meaningful experience comes from a perfect balance between the volitional ego and the non-volitional self."
    – Pathwork Lecture #142

So how did we get here? If we look around, we can see evidence of creativity in the way life is constantly moving, changing and branching into new territories. This is what leads to individualization. But over time, as we've experienced ourselves as ego-based individuals, we've drifted further and further from the source at our center and forgotten our essence. Eventually we only associate ourselves with our separate existence—with our ego.

From here, with the ego firmly in the lead, we will fear letting go of the outer ego because we do not want to lose our sense of identity. We feel threatened by this feeling of "I am not," and we hold on more tightly. Hence the ego must become strong enough to relax to let go of itself; it has to become brave enough to die to its own illusion. This is what needs to happen for us to experience our connection with all that is and to live in the Oneness. Again, this is where we all must go.

For the truth is, we really are one with the creative nature of life, meaning we can surrender to this greater force and allow our ego functions to integrate with it. Then, when we are in touch with our real self—which means we are in unity within ourselves—we will have access to feeling, experiencing and knowing deeply, which is to be creative.

The ego, on the other hand, can't embrace opposites, meaning it cannot transcend duality and find peace. So then peace without the experience of excitement will feel like boredom, while excitement without peace will mean anxiety. Living primarily from the ego then, as most humans do, makes one feel perpetually bored or anxious.

"Ego means effort; spiritual self means effortlessness. This desirable effortlessness is not given by magic, however, for this would mean that the ego is not being transcended but avoided. The ego must change its lazy, resistant attitudes in order to transcend itself—to become able to unify with the cosmic, greater self."
    – Pathwork Lecture #199

To transcend our ego, we must make an effort to align with our spiritual self where all effort can feel effortless. But such desirable effortlessness is not handed out like candy. The ego must work for it, overcoming its lazy ways and resistant attitudes.

Further, we must come to see that it is possible to experience this universal power in the present moment, and not wait for a fulfillment that is pushed off—as religions often promote—into life after death. Ironically, the ego would prefer to wait, given the great misunderstanding that giving up the ego means giving up existence. As a result, the ego cramps up in response to the movement of letting go, making the unfoldment of happiness impossible.

Some spiritual teachings say the ego should be dispensed with. But nothing could be further from the truth. The ego has a job to do and it needs to get moving. Which is to say, it must wake up, know its position, and establish permanent contact with the greater self. It is also tasked with discovering the obstructions between it and the real self, taking action to open the doors that allow the Higher Self to heal the Lower Self.

"After it has fulfilled its task of deciding for truthfulness, integrity, honesty, effort and good will, it must step aside and allow the real self to come forth with its intuition and inspiration that set the pace and direct the individual path…The ego can be likened to hands and arms that move toward the source of life and stop moving when their function is no longer anything else but to receive."
– Pathwork Lecture #158

Living life from the ego is exhausting, because the ego cannot replenish itself at the source. If the ego can let go, it can be reenergized through sleep, which is a rest from ego chores. But when the ego is overactive, sleep is often fitful. Self-forgetfulness also happens in the state of love for another person, making it possible for the ego to dip into the sea of replenishing power. Another way is through deep meditation, where one surrenders to greater truths, new wisdom opens up inner doors and our whole being can be rejuvenated.

Since there's so much to be gained, why doesn't the ego just let go? Because it is hazardous to let go as long as the ego is immature and unhealthy.

If the ego is nurturing hate, distrust, weakness and a tendency for self-damaging behaviors, it is not compatible with the greater reality which runs on being loving, generous, open, trusting, realistic and self-assertive.

As long as we're not equipped to take care of ourselves and we let our ego engage in behaviors that go against the best interest of our whole being, we're in no shape to let go. For our weak unhealthy ego will then become unsupported, totally disorganized and unable to cope with anything. This is why our destructiveness must be given up.

So if we feel unable to let go, somewhere in us is a will to be negative and destructive. The Lower Self is ruling the roost. This destructiveness includes being vindictive, not loving others, and punishing others for our suffering. But no one is forcing us to give anything up against our will. We must be the ones who take the necessary steps to give up destructiveness.

We spend as much as 95% of our time in our ego, unbalanced and with life lacking meaning. The unhealed ego knows it doesn't have solutions, but it doesn't yet know another way.

"To the extent these experiences are hindered because of obstruction in the personality which the ego is unwilling to remove, to that extent life dries out and various degrees of death set in. Actual physical death is the natural end result of a process of drying out, of separating the self from the source of all life."
– Pathwork Lecture #161

In its unhealed state, the basic message coming from the ego is "See me, I'm better than you, love me for it," as it acts out the Lower Self qualities of self-will, pride and fear. The ego fears its own death and denies the Higher Self, using its distrust to justify staying separate. The ego must overcome its fear of death, lower its pride, and let go to the greater consciousness.

To avoid this, the ego will use tricks such as inattentiveness, lack of concentration or absent-mindedness to prevent the focusing necessary for the ego to transcend itself. Laziness, tiredness and passivity are other tricks of the ego. They make movement impossible, undesirable and exhausting. The unhealed ego will also allow its own immature emotional reactions to go unchecked, and make more of another's behavior than necessary.

To transcend itself, the ego must be able to focus. It needs discipline, courage, humility and the ability to commit itself. Our goal is for the ego to become mature and healed, not denied or insulted. The searchlight of truth must be directed on the little self, recognizing these tricks for what they are. Denial, rationalization and projection must be given up. Only in this way can we adopt healthy, truthful attitudes.

We are in turmoil because we rebel against what is unchangeable: people don't respond or behave the way we want them to; situations don't go the way we had hoped. Life isn't perfect and we won't surrender to what is. We trust the limited ego instead of letting go and trusting the God that lives within.

Prayer

> Use me God.
> Show me how to take
> Who I am,
> Who I want to be, and
> What I can do,
> And use it for a purpose
> Greater than myself.
> – Martin Luther King Jr.

Learn more in *After the Ego: Insights from the Pathwork® Guide on How to Wake Up*.

The Guide teaches in the very first lecture that spiritual laws can be made a living reality on three different levels: doing, thinking and feeling. The easiest to deal with is actions, which is where the ego is most effective. This is the level mankind was mostly operating at when God gave us the Ten Commandments, including "Thou shalt not steal" and "Thou shalt not lie." That was a lot to take in for the average person at that time.

The next stage deals with our thoughts. All thoughts and feelings have form and substance in the Spirit World. In not understanding this, we think our impure thoughts won't hurt us. We would be wrong. They do bring about outer effects and chain reactions. But we have to start somewhere, and so we can often "act our way into right thinking," at least in some areas.

The most difficult task is on the emotional level. This is hard because many feelings are unconscious and we need work, willpower and patience to make them conscious. Further, we can't control our feelings as immediately and directly as our thoughts or actions. We can force ourselves to walk this path but we can't will ourselves to love or have the faith that will come as a result of our work on this path.

The ability to surrender is an essential inner movement from which all good can flow. Over time, which may take thousands of years and many lifetimes, the ego will dissolve into the greater consciousness. We need to surrender to the will of God or else we will be shortsighted, in pain and confusion, and in our self-will.

We also need to surrender to others—our teachers, healers and loved ones. Refusal to surrender means lack of trust and a suspicion and misunderstanding that surrender means loss of autonomy and the ability to make future decisions. This creates an over-developed self-will that always brings strife. We need to find the balance between holding firm and surrendering. It is not a contradiction.

- Where in our life are we standing in our active, positive aggression?
- Where are we able to let go and trust?
- Where have we let go into futility and hopelessness?
- Where do we defend tightly, refusing to give in?
- Where do we lack self-responsibility?
- Where are we secretly dependent, yet outwardly defiantly independent?
- Where is the hidden corner of ourselves that we withhold?
- Where do we genuinely surrender?
- Where do we surrender falsely, to please others?
- Where do we want to be superior?
- Where do we hold back our greatness?

Learn more in *Gems*, Chapter 4: Claiming our Total Capacity for Greatness, and Chapter 10: Spotting the Tricks of our Ego and Getting Over Ourselves.

It is suggested in feng shui that if we want something new to come into our life, we should clean out our closets. In a similar way, the Guide teaches that our psyches are like a vessel. If they are filled with muddy water and we pour in clear water, the clear water will become muddy too. So we must empty ourselves of the muddy water first, which means to understand its contents, such as misconceptions. Then the truth behind the untruth can be set free.

When we trust the limited ego instead of God within, we set up a duality: use a forcing current to "get" versus resignation into hopelessness. This stops the flow of light, truth, love, abundance and fulfillment. What we need to let go of is the limited ego and its self-will and narrow understanding.

We also need to let go of fears, distrust, suspicions, misconceptions, insistent demands on how life should be, and even our legitimate wants for something precious. This is referred to in first Beatitude, which Jesus Christ gave in his Sermon on the Mount: "Blessed are the poor in spirit, for theirs is the kingdom of heaven."

To be "poor in spirit" means to be empty, without preconceived ideas. Our minds are often "rich" in the wrong way—we know all the answers. But our knowledge often stems from associations based on misunderstandings, products of fixed ideas based on faulty and emotionally tinged associations.

Only when we can empty ourselves of our preconceived notions can we become "poor in spirit," or in mind. And then the true riches can flow into us—from within and without.

"Being at ease with not knowing is crucial for answers to come to you."
– Eckhart Tolle

Realize that material wealth does not need to be a hindrance to spiritual wealth. It often can be, just as other kinds of power can be, but if knowledge is used to deny the Holy Spirit, it is as much of an obstruction as money or any other kind of wealth can be.

The key is to let go and trust. First, we must trust that the universe is benign and giving—we can have the best. Second, we are not required to suffer. We can learn to "let God" from the center of our being where God speaks to us, if we choose to listen. It cannot be done once—it must be experienced many, many times. We may lose trust in buckets, but it can only be gained in droplets.

With time, we'll become willing to let go of our demands for immediate gratification and for the world to show up perfectly; we build spiritual muscle when we can do this. We'll let go of our need to be special and we'll discover the richness of being part of a greater reality.

"Desperation results from the tightness that shuts God out, not from not having what you want."
– Pathwork Lecture #213

Learn more in *Pearls*, Chapter 17: Discovering the Key to Letting Go & Letting God, and *Gems*, Chapter 15: Surrendering to the Double-Sided Nature of Duality.

PART III: DOING THE WORK

The journey of a soul can be likened to water. What began as a vapor gradually turned to the solid denseness of ice—not from some random act of fate but due to our own choices. Over time, we began to long for another way of being, and so we have begun the long journey back to the Oneness. We no longer want to experience ourselves as separate snowflakes.

Life and spiritual laws are exquisitely designed to bring us back home. When we begin to thaw, the water of our being is cloudy and still frozen in many places. Even as we believe ourselves to be victims of a senseless unfair universe, we begin to learn the truth about how we constantly defend ourselves and unknowingly bring about our current life circumstances. We can make new choices and the water will begin to clear.

Bit by bit, we come out of the trance we have been in. We begin to see cause and effect, and to take responsibility for the state of our lives. Gradually, our lives transform. The water warms and begins to evaporate. We once again can sense our essential nature and eternal connectedness with all that is.

In the course of this work, we develop on various levels of our being. In our spirit, we move from the separation of duality to unity. In our mind, we move from images and vicious circles to truth. In our will, we move from forcing currents and withholding, to receptivity and a willingness to give.

In our emotions, we move from being blocked and numb, to being flowing and changing. In our bodies, we move from being frozen and split, to being open, breathing and integrated.

Following is an overview of the work we can do to heal our souls.

Overview of Doing the Work of Healing | The Way Out

- Something triggers an **Emotional Reaction**

    Bring reason to our emotions to discover the cause.

- Come out of **Blame** and being a **Victim**

    Take responsibility for seeing cause and effect in ourselves.

- **Pray & Meditate** to see the truth

    Use mature ego to connect with Higher Self.

- Find the **Image**

    Clearly express the statement of the belief.

- Release **Residual Pain**

    Feel the pain of unmet needs.

- Find the **Duality**

    See the misconception and open to seeing reality.

- Feel and unwind the **Forcing Current**

    Or find the collapse into hopelessness.

- Connect with **Negative Pleasure**

    Discover the pleasure in being destructive.

- Recognize **Faults**

    Reveal the triad of pride, fear and self-will.

- Transform **Negative Intention**

    Find where we need to give.

- Search for a **No-Current**

  Find faulty thinking that undermines fulfillment.

- Uncover **Real Needs**

  Pray and meditate to connect with our longing.

- Impress soul substance with **New Awareness**

  Re-educate the inner child with the truth.

- Pray for **Healing**

  Divine energy fills and heals the wound.

Over time, we will develop discernment and a truer perception about the world around us. We will shift from our defensiveness, to a stance of openness and transparency. The emotional reactions of others may affect us, but that doesn't mean they activate us. We will be wise in our self-disclosure and rigorous in self-honesty. We will learn to become vulnerable and we will know peace.

Calling on God | Prayer & Meditation

A s we do this work, we will come to know, through our own experiences, that what we experience is a reflection of what we believe. We
will have this "knowing" because we will embody this truth, and not just
know about it.

Another truth we can come to know is that life is abundant. If that is not
our current experience, we cannot just wish for what we want. We must
eliminate the obstructions, which include images, faults and negative intention. The tools for doing this are prayer & meditation.

Meaningful meditation is a way to: check, test and challenge our concepts; seek truth and adjust our ideas and aims to it; and purify our
feelings by going through them. We can even use meditation to uncover
what we should meditate about, or to help eliminate what prevents us
from meditating.

As we progress through various stages of our journey, our relationship
with prayer and meditation evolves. We begin in a place of being without
awareness, where there is no prayer and no concept of God. As we begin
to wake up and get curious about life, our wondering is the prayer and
meditation.

We move to a realization of a supreme intelligence, perhaps from marveling at science or nature. Here we experience an admiration that is a form of worship. These progressions of course are not linear.

With this sense of God outside ourselves, we experience confusion, immaturity, and feelings of inadequacy that cause fear, clinging, helplessness, wishful thinking and greed. Our prayers are then petitions to this God outside of us.

From here we move into a more independent phase of atheism. There is no prayer to God, but we may look at ourselves sincerely. Or we may escape both God and the self through irresponsibility.

We gradually come to face the self and to develop self-awareness. There is more candor with the self and we become alert to our resistance, uncovering what feels shameful. All this creates an attitude that is the prayer. Slowly we arrive at a state of being, living in the eternal Now with love and awareness of God. This is the natural outcome of facing the self.

Creation requires the presence of both the active and the passive principles. The active is masculine and it is the "make it happen" energy. The passive, or receptive, is feminine and it is the "let it happen" energy. Both are needed for creation to happen. So to use prayer and meditation to create, we must combine intelligent thinking, which is the active prayer, with relaxing and listening to the divine, which is the receptive meditation.

We can learn concentration and discipline in the active state of prayer, cleansing our thoughts and getting clear about what we want help with. We do this by looking at every disharmony, no matter how insignificant, and asking: Where did I have negative feelings? What did I feel? Why did I feel that?

Then we use these qualities of concentration and discipline to sit in the silence and emptiness of meditation, listening. To be in balance, we should always turn our focus towards the one we find most difficult.

Four Steps for Prayer & Meditation

Concept | Active
- Clarify thoughts; remove obstacles.
- Conceive of new possibilities.
- Face the truth, feel feelings.

Impress Soul Substance | Receptive
- Relax inner will; remove defenses.
- Uncover unconscious currents.
- Allow inner truth, love, wisdom to surface.
- Drop in a seed and let it germinate.
  - o Do not disrupt it with doubt, fear, impatience.

Visualization
- Feel ourselves in the state we want to be in.
  - o Without particulars.

Faith
- We cannot superimpose this.
- Have patience and examine doubts.

"Become very still and say these words inside of yourself: Be still and know I am God, the ultimate power. Listen to this power within, to this presence and to these intentions. I am God, everyone is God. God is all, in everything that lives and moves, that breathes and knows, that feels and is.

God in me has the power to make the separated little ego know the ultimate power to integrate this ego. I have the possibility to feel all my feelings—to deal with and handle all my feelings. This possibility is there in me, and I know this potentiality can be realized the moment I know it. And I now choose to know I can be alive; I have the strength to be weak and vulnerable.

I can accept my numbness now, my insecurities, my feeling state and my nonfeeling state. I can listen into this state and wait. I can be still and feel into me. I can be still and hear my superior intelligence, the God intelligence, instruct me. I can establish this contact.

I will pay the price by giving the best I have and am to life. I will live my life honestly in wanting to give the best. For then I will be able to receive the best without cringing. I do not fear to invest the best of myself into life."

– The Pathwork Guide in Q&A #201

Learn more in *Pearls*, Chapter 2: Reading Between the Lines of the Lord's Prayer, and in *Bones*, Chapter 18: How to Use Meditation to Create a Better Life.

Before we can be filled with joyful, positive creation, we must empty ourselves of our negativity and the rulership of the little ego. The ego mind, which is the self we most often identify with, is sustained by the "activity" by which it tries to accumulate knowledge and be in control. It is therefore afraid of emptiness, because in emptiness, it does not exist.

On a spiritual path, we eventually must come face to face with this terror. If we don't, we will perpetually deceive ourselves as to the nature of reality—and to the ultimate nature of the real self.

Instead, we often identify with the busyness of the mind, and mistake the absence of busyness for emptiness. There are three paradoxes that must be accepted for creation to take place:

1. If one cannot tolerate emptiness, one will never be filled.
2. One must be expectant and receptive without preconceived ideas or wishful thinking.
3. One needs to be specific in his or her longing and expectations, yet this specificity must be light and neutral.

Learn more in *After the Ego*, Chapter 12: Creating from Emptiness, and Chapter 17: Inner Space, Focused Emptiness.

Lifting the Lid | Shame

W hen we begin to do this work, we may start to think it is creating problems for us. In truth, our difficulties are not caused by this work of self-inquiry. They result from our unresolved pains that hide in our areas of blindness. So if we want to uncover our deepest problems—to heal our deepest wounds—we need to go where we haven't wanted to look. The access route is through our shame.

There are actually two kinds of shame—a right kind and a wrong kind. The right kind is true repentance. Without this kind of shame, there would be no incentive for self-development, and we wouldn't take on this noble fight against our Lower Self.

The wrong kind of shame says, "I am hopelessly bad, and there is nothing that can be done about it." Our lack of self-respect is not due to our shortcomings—no matter what they may be. It is due to having the wrong kind of shame.

Learn more in *Living Light*, Chapter 14: SHAME | The Right and Wrong Kind.

Shame is essentially the word we use to describe the feeling of needing to keep down—or out of our awareness—the blind spots we are afraid to see, or to let others see. It is a trick used by our ego that does not want to be exposed, and acts like a tight lid that cautions us to keep looking away.

Shame is the outer layer of our mask, and so when we embark on any path of self-healing, it is the first thing we bump into. But once we work up the courage to reveal ourselves to another, the shame lifts off.

Until that happens, shame will keep us from knowing if we are ever really loved and appreciated. For this little voice in us says, "If they only knew how I really am and what I have done, they would not love me." Then any affection we receive seems destined for the person we appear to be, not the person we are. We end up feeling insecure and lonely.

We can begin to heal when we admit the aspects that cause shame, such as fear of appearing less than others, fear of belittlement, and fear of humiliation. When we take the risk to share these fears with others, we'll often see we're not alone—our fears and faults are basically the same as everyone else's.

"Most people are motivated to start spiritual work like this because what they really seek are better ways to avoid the undesirable feelings. When it finally dawns on them that exactly the opposite direction must be taken, many leave the path, unwilling to accept the truth that avoidance is futile. They insist on their illusion."

– Pathwork Lecture #191

Once we take the first steps to courageously look into our hidden areas—and allow ourselves to feel the vulnerability that comes with that—we will see shame for what it is. It is part of an illusion that keeps us in separation—from ourselves, from others and from knowing God. In the end, the illusion is that we can avoid whatever exists in us.

Therefore the road to self-respect does not require we be free of our faults—to be perfect. Self-respect comes by adopting a realistic and constructive attitude toward our imperfections. This is why the basic requirement to be on this path is to be honest with ourselves, and to not desire to appear better than we are.

Learn more in *Pearls*, Chapter 1: Privacy vs. Secrecy: A Boost or Bust for Finding Closeness, and Chapter 9: Why Flubbing on Perfection is the Way to Find Joy.

The Guide explains that we can also experience shame about the best and noblest part of ourselves—our Higher Self. Here's how this comes about. Every child would like to be loved and approved of to a much greater extent than is possible, particularly by the parent who seems to reject it—imagined or real does not matter. When this exclusive affection doesn't happen, the child feels it as a rejection.

The desired aim—exclusive love and acceptance—is then confused with the parent withholding it. In the immature mind of the child, the rejecter now becomes desirable, taking the place of that which was originally desired.

Therefore the child concludes that to be unloving is a desirable state. Then being cold, aloof and free of emotions—the behavior pattern of the rejecter—becomes the strategy for no longer being rejected. With this in the unconscious, the adult then feels it is shameful to demonstrate love.

While it is easy to see that the logic is faulty, it also has its own quite understandable limited logic in the child's mind. This is the type of wrong thinking that needs to be surfaced and examined.

Learn more in *Living Light*, Chapter 15: SHAME OF THE HIGHER SELF | We're Ashamed of Our Best Self. Crazy, Right?

Mining Our Thoughts | Images

A ll experiences begin with thoughts, because in thought lies intent. Thoughts and beliefs create feelings, which lead to attitudes and behaviors, and this is what results in life circumstances. So in making changes, we always have to begin with our thoughts. The problem lies in our not actually knowing what we really think and believe.

When we look out over the ocean, we see the waves and the birds and the boats and swimmers and the islands. But for the most part, we cannot see what lies under the surface. It is like that with our thoughts that have gone into our unconscious. They are out of sight, but they are not out of mind.

When a child has a painful experience, it feels like life and death. To avoid death, the child will draw conclusions about life that are intended to keep it safe. The Guide calls our many wrong conclusions "images." They are generalizations about life that are primitive, ignorant and illogical, although they follow a certain logic of their own.

As the child grows older, these unconscious thoughts don't hold up to the light of day. So they sink into the unconscious where they have great power to do damage, attracting disappointing life experiences that are often the exact opposite from what is consciously desired. These images are what we need to surface if we want to understand the root of any unfulfilling patterns in our lives.

Images are formed when a child is quite young, so they are usually constructed with a child's vocabulary. "People want to be mean to me" is an example. This is a generalized conclusion that a child of an aggressive Will Type parent might believe to be true about everyone.

This person then goes through life unconsciously believing that everyone is a potential enemy. Consciously, they just want people to be nice to them. But due to this image, the person will show up defended behind a mask. Then, when the other, due to their own issues—or perhaps in reaction to being presented with an impenetrable mask—is unkind, it will feel like the threat of death, confirming the image and the need for the defense.

This underground dynamic causes a person to go through life in a trance that narrows their perception of reality. Not seeing the whole truth, life situations are erroneously interpreted to be intentionally hurtful, and the person reacts accordingly.

This explains how in our blindness, we continually recreate life experiences that seem to validate our misconceptions. When these beliefs surface, there will be a recognition that says, "Yes, this is what I have always believed was true." So we are not searching for some idea that will seem completely foreign to us. Yet, until we surface it, it will remain just beyond our grasp.

Learn more in *Bones*, Chapter 9: Images and the Deep, Deep Damage They Do.

Images create an inflexible, rigid mass in the soul substance that will stay with us until we begin to do this work of self-understanding. Only by surfacing all of this can we see how our unconscious desires conflict with what we think we want.

So why wouldn't we all immediately dive in and discover what lurks below the waterline? Pride—that's what stops us. We don't want to be wrong, because in the dualistic way of thinking, being wrong is bad. And for the child, that seems to confirm being worthless.

Surprisingly, just seeing these hidden beliefs does not stop them from operating. We need to be willing to feel the associated buried feelings so we can stop defending against the threat of pain. And we need to employ our healthy ego to access our inner self to find the truth of the matter.

Then we can begin the gradual process of re-educating and maturing the inner child: "It is not true that people intend to be mean to me. Sometimes they lash out due to their own issues, but this does not mean that they are personally out to get me. I can use my communication skills to ask questions and seek to understand the other."

The Prayer of Saint Francis

Lord, make me an instrument of thy peace.
Where there is hatred, let me sow love;
Where there is injury, pardon;
Where there is doubt, faith;
Where there is despair, hope;
Where there is darkness, light;
Where there is sadness, joy.

O divine Master, grant that I may not so much seek
To be consoled as to console,
To be understood as to understand,
To be loved as to love;
For it is in giving that we receive;
It is in pardoning that we are pardoned;
It is in dying to self that we are born to eternal life.

Our Lower Self wants to always have its way, without ever having to pay any price for this. It is a spiritual law, however, that to have what we want in life, there is a price we must be willing to pay. The price is self-confrontation. Alternatively, living a life in which emotional reactions or negative patterns of behavior repeatedly happen is the price we pay for our beliefs that go against truth.

The spiritual Law of Brotherhood says we don't have to do this work alone, and that more help is given when we reach out to another. To see our own blindness, we often need the patience, skill and guiding hand of someone else—perhaps a therapist or a trained spiritual healer—who can help hold the flashlight while we look into these hidden inner spaces.

Origin of an Image | A Process of Four Steps

1. Childhood hurts cause unhappiness and discontent, and the child wants to avoid pain.
2. Child concludes that each similar situation to the one that caused the hurt will bring similar pain. So what was once a reality has now turned into an illusion because the generalization is false.
3. The generalization freezes into a rigid preconceived idea. This is the image: a frozen wrong conception, an inflexible, rigid mass in the soul substance, which attracts situations to justify its continued existence.
4. As the image is unreal, so must be the "remedy" or pseudo-solution which is adopted. Because it is unrealistic, the results are disappointing, often producing the exact opposite from what is desired. So the circumstances continue to be produced.

Dismantling an Image | A Process of Four Steps

1. Find the statement of the image, and write it out in black and white. For example: I don't matter; I am worthless; I cause other people pain; People will always be mean to me; Nobody likes me; I have to prove myself; I'm not enough and I will never be enough.
2. Connect with the willingness to consciously find the original event where the pain was felt. Feel that old pain by letting go of the pride which prevents the experience of feeling the hurt.
3. Be willing to challenge the original conclusion and see what the right conclusion could be.
4. Pray for the truth to be revealed. Allow the new conclusion to be planted in the newly alive soil of our opened feelings.

Learn more in *Healing the Hurt: How to Help Using Spiritual Guidance.*

Revealing the Face | The God Image

Practically everything a child enjoys most is forbidden. Therefore authority is the very first conflict for a growing child. The child also learns that God is the highest authority. Therefore, pleasure equals punishment from God. This makes a monster out of God, although it's really more of a Satan. This is often the reason for atheism. One fears a God who is severe, unjust, pious, self-righteous and cruel.

The origin of this stems from the child's reaction to his or her parents. If the child received strict discipline, the reaction to the parents may be hostile. The reaction to God then is fear and frustration, believing God to be punishing, severe and unfair. The attitude towards life then is one of hopelessness and despair, believing the universe to be unjust.

If the parents were indulgent, the child's reaction will be more benign, but the child may believe it can get away with anything and avoid self-responsibility. The belief is in a pampering universe.

In our work, we need to become aware of what we believe and that it is false. Then we can formulate a right concept, which we need inner enlightenment to see. The truth is that we are the one obstructing the light and freedom, not God.

Learn more in *Bones*, Chapter 14: Exposing the Mistaken Image We have About God, and in *Pearls*, Chapter 10: Two Rebellious Reactions to Authority.

God's laws are infinitely good, wise, loving and safe, and they make us wholly free and independent. They always lead to light and bliss. The pain created by any deviation becomes the medicine that leads to the cure. But we have free will to choose our way.

God is not a person who acts with justice. God is life and life force—like an electric current with supreme intelligence. God's laws work automatically, so the great creative power current is always at our disposal.

If we experience an injustice, we need to find our part—whether it is ignorance, fear, pride or egotism. According to the Law of Cause and Effect, our unconscious affects others' unconscious. So our attitude, deeds, thoughts and emotions all matter.

"The particular path on which I lead you, my dear friends, will make you understand, step by step, how and where your outer problems are connected to your inner conflicts, where you react emotionally in a way that will attract certain happenings to you as inevitably as a magnet draws iron to itself.

These forces can be truly understood only when you uncover your emotions and find out their deeper meaning. And with that knowledge you find the particular reason and purpose of your life, your own individual existence.

When this is discovered, an entity has reached an important phase in his or her whole cycle of incarnations. That this knowledge can be brought forth is the result of important efforts, which in turn are a sign that a soul has reached a significant milestone on the upward road.

At that point you step across the borderline between unconsciousness and consciousness with a higher degree of awareness. The true understanding of one's present existence marks, indeed, a major stepping stone of a soul's return journey to God."

– Pathwork Lecture #46

Learn more in *Spiritual Laws: Hard & Fast Logic for Forging Ahead.*

Freeing the Force | One Energy

We have the mistaken belief that we can freeze or avoid our unpleasant feelings, and then live life enjoying just the good ones. If only it worked that way. In truth, if we freeze one feeling, we freeze them all. The result is a numbed out life of overall flatness.

Pure Higher Self life force is totally positive, constructive and affirming. Lower Self is a distortion of Higher Self, which it works hard to repress. Negative emotions then cannot be replaced by positive emotions—they must be transformed.

Interestingly, the Guide tells us that we often have a greater fear of pleasure than of pain. The key in learning to tolerate pleasure is to learn to endure what is inside right now, which could include meanness, resentment, spite, jealousy, guilt, rage or terror.

It can feel painful to be with these uncomfortable feelings. We need to let them be present and held by the light of Higher Self. When we do, we can see that anxiety is really just suppressed excitement. Panic is really fear of fear. If we stop breathing, it can become fear of suffocating. Underneath, it's really just energy, or excitement. Boredom is stifled energy that feels numb instead of anxious. Pleasure unfolds organically as a byproduct of going through the darkness within.

When we release our blocked emotions and rewire our misguided thoughts to align with truth, we will feel an incredible infusion of new strength, resourcefulness and creative abilities. We are literally unwinding an aspect of negativity so that it can organically return to its higher energy state, and we can get our life force back.

So our intention is not to cut off or get rid of the Lower Self—it is alive and therefore is part of our real self. We want to convert it. In this way, for instance, we can learn from the Lower Self voice, finding perception and discernment in place of judgment. Our goal is to return all our distorted aspects to their original face—through which shines the face of God.

Learn more in *Bones*, Chapter 1: Emotional Growth and Its Function, and Chapter 2: The Importance of Feeling All Our Feelings, Including Fear.

Reversing the Flow | Negative Pleasure

T he Guide teaches that life and pleasure are the same—people cannot live without pleasure. So when, as children, we found ourselves experiencing unpleasant feelings, we attached our pleasure current to the unpleasant experience. This is the crossing of pleasure and pain.

We then go through life unknowingly recreating this same unpleasant experience so we can activate our life force. This is why negativity is so hard to shed—it contains pleasure.

If the feeling was frustration, we will recreate frustration. If the atmosphere was chaotic, we will recreate chaos. If the pattern was need-rejection-collapse, we will recreate "I am hurt—I collapse to stop the pain."

If we felt bullied, we will recreate that. A bully will hurt until the other gives in and they break through. The pleasure is in the intense contact. We need to find the pleasure in the destruction, seeing how we are electrified by a negative pleasure.

Our negative situations generate tension fields of energy. We may not know what life would be like without these humming around us. As with our childhood environment, they may feel like the water a fish swims in—they are just always there.

It takes some maturity to be able to tolerate a negative tension field while working to dismantle it. Otherwise, we may use various ways—such as eating, drinking, smoking, spending or gambling—to numb or distract ourselves from them. These pseudo-pleasures may feel like short-term relief from the tension—and these things may even deliver a hit of "aliveness"—but then they create more problems from which we hope to escape.

We can ask the question, "How do I get my life force activated?" Then we need to find the positive pleasure in this and reconvert this into a benign circle. It is actually powerful to align with God's will, and we can cultivate that positive pleasure. As Keith Covington put it, "When we walk through the doorway of Christ, we become the door."

Learn more in *Living Light*, Chapter 2: MOBILITY IN RELAXATION | Could this be the Answer...to Everything? and in *Bones*, Chapter 16: How Pleasure Gets Twisted into Self-Perpetuating Cycles of Pain.

Unwinding the Worst | Faults

The Guide teaches that whenever there is any disharmony within us—no matter how wrong the other may be—there is something in us we overlook. It is an error though to believe that if we go on a spiritual path such as this one, bad things won't happen in our life.

This is an imperfect world. People will continue to do imperfect things. And bad things will happen. It is how we respond to them that makes all the difference. Pain is inevitable, but suffering is optional.

In the end, the only thing we can change is ourselves. But sometimes that changes everything. To making substantial and lasting changes though, we need to be willing to look closely at all aspects of ourselves. This path is not a bolt-on addition to our lives—it is a shift to a new set of tracks. We have already wasted many lifetimes and some of our issues have become tight knots, but they can be loosened and unraveled with patience and good work.

The key in doing this work is to learn to identify the areas of distortion within ourselves, but not identify with them. Whatever it is, it is not all of us. And it is definitely not the core essence of who we are.

All human beings have faults, which are places in us that are in distortion. Our faults serve separation and not connection, and that is how we know they belong under the umbrella of Lower Self. Because they are part of the domain of Lower Self, all faults fall into one of three main categories: self-will, pride or fear. Pride encompasses both the attitudes of being better than and less than—we wouldn't have to make ourselves seem better than if we didn't feel like we are less than—and is the opposite of humility. Just naming pride, once we identify it, is often all that's needed to let go of it.

Fear is an emotion, so if we feel it, it changes. We can "smell" it in another, but once we resolve our own, it will open up our intuition. We need to learn to "feel the fear and do it anyway," which is essentially a little ego-death experience. Fear breeds resistance and resistance breeds fear, including fear of truth which then negates the real self, which is truth.

Self-will is a compulsive forcing current that does not come from a free act, but rather from a feeling of "I should, I must, I ought to." It is a superficial current of tension, anxiety and pushing. Healthy will is free and relaxed, acting for the sake of truth and integrity.

This triad can always be found together, so when we identify a fault in one of these areas, we can be sure the other two are lurking nearby. It is always good to look for all three once we identify any fault. According to one's Personality Type, one of these will likely be easiest to find: self-will for the Will Type, pride for the Reason Type, and fear for the Emotion Type.

Learn more in *Bones*, Chapter 12: Finding Out the Truth about Ourselves, Including Our Faults, and Chapter 13: The Ubiquitous Faults of Self-Will, Pride and Fear.

Let's look more closely at our fear. While it's true we need to be able to stand up for ourselves—even defend ourselves, when necessary—we don't need to be in fear to do this. More to the point, it's our fear that prevents us from doing this effectively.

Fear is that feeling in our gut that tells us something out there is going to hurt us. It casts a net over everything we see, looking for a scene that is somehow reminiscent of something hurtful that happened back when, probably in our childhood. "Aha,'" it says, "I've spotted it. See, I needed my fear to keep me safe."

Armed with this type of defensive strategy, we walk through life in a trance, seeing the world through a hypersensitive filter. This perpetual pinging of everything crossing our path keeps our system on semi-alert, and keeps us in an elevated state of perceived stress. Our physical body joins this hunt for hurtful things by constantly dumping low doses of cortisol into our blood. Just in case. Because, you never know. We might need it. At any moment.

But cortisol does things to the body, like reducing bone formation—think: osteoporosis—and weakening the immune system—think: get sick. Worse yet, should we find ourselves in need of our God-given ability to think and defend ourselves in a truly unsafe situation, all this "preparation" has made us less capable. Because when we're living in fear, we're running on a half-fried system.

Fear arises from that part of ourselves that wants us to stay separate, and to stay very afraid. The Lower Self whispers in our ear about a past that haunts us, and uses this to keep us out of our current reality. It leverages our own buried wrong conclusions so that our attitudes and actions cause monsters to materialize.

This is how we create our own frightful reality, then turn around and claim it was our fear that kept us safe. The way out is by finding the courage to face the ghosts of our own hidden painful past. We must unravel our fears if we want to quench that anxiety in our gut.

Learn more about facing fear in *Blinded by Fear: Insights from the Pathwork Guide on How to Face our Fears*.

Perhaps the most important thing to know about faults is that they are always a distortion of an original divine essence. The pride, fear and self-will inherent in every human being will eventually give way to humility, love and the willingness to have God's will done in all respects. So we want to unearth them and reconvert them to their original glory. Following are a few negative qualities and their original divine essence:

Defiance; Spite; Stubbornness; Rigidity | Being centered within; Being firm, self-assertive and standing our own ground; Being secure in our own self, rather than being constantly swayed and influenced by others and thus losing autonomy.

Rebelliousness; Going against authority | Courage and independence; A fighting spirit against submission to conformity.

Abuse of power, of a position of authority | True leadership, which means taking responsibility and paying the price for leadership.

Judge others | Great capacity to distinguish, to differentiate; Honestly and constructively see the truth in ourselves, with keen perception of others; Recognition.

Lack of faith; Do not want to believe in God | Healthy, realistic attitude regarding self-responsibility and self-dependence; Know that there is no authority that will do it for us; Surrender of the ego to the deeper, wiser Godself to bring about true selfhood, autonomy, independence; Willingness to keep all doors open in search for truth.

Fearfulness; Anxiety | Caution; Awareness that something is amiss; Anxiety is a gauge that tells us something is being repressed that we don't wish to see.

Avoid taking responsibility for one's life | Quality of letting go and letting flow, of not letting the ego-control take over and blot out the eternal flow of being; Not being cramped and tight and overactive with the ego forces; Giving in and surrendering to the flow of being.

Playing the victim game; Self-exoneration at the expense of making others guilty | Longing for the perfect state we contain in our nucleus, which is not a fixed perfectionism, but the ever-moving, changing perfection of the innermost soul.

Competitiveness; Self-centeredness; Wanting to be the center of attention; Vanity; Egotism | Centered within our divine self, not the separated ego; Being the best that we can be.

Removing ourselves; Being "cool;" Pretending to be different | Self-containment, self-sufficiency, impartiality, serenity; Harmonious balance between intimate sharing and solitude to refuel from within.

Compulsion of telling jokes | Life is joyous, pleasurable, lighthearted, humorous; There cannot be beauty and love without humor.

If we are not aware of our faults, or character defects, consider this a good opportunity to begin to get to know ourselves better. We can do this work of self-discovery by asking someone who knows us well to sit down and tell us what they think our good qualities are, as well as our faults.

This is truly a sacred gift if someone is willing to take the risk of dropping into such honesty with us. We need to do our best to just receive, without defending or rebutting. And know that some of the others' issues could be coloring some of what they say. Still, what a gift to be shown how another perceives us.

Our deeply entrenched faults have been with us for many lifetimes, so they won't dissolve in a day. And they won't resolve themselves just because we know about them. We need to bring our healthy will to bear on the situation, identifying them in action and taking steps to make another choice. Doing this requires rigorous self-honesty.

As we go through our list of faults, we will see that we really do not like some of them. But others, we sort of cherish in some way. When we see such an attachment, we can ask: "How would I react if another person were to display the same fault, either in the same way or perhaps in a slightly different way?" In fact, we are often quite irritated when someone else displays the same fault we are somewhat proud of. This will help loosen the pride we take in our fault. We also rid ourselves of pride when we have the courage to stumble a thousand times over the same faults and forever lift ourselves up to try again. Then we are truly on this path.

"Our greatest glory is not in never falling, but in rising every time we fall."

– Confucius

The Guide tells us when spirits observe human beings, they can see how badly we need spiritual nourishment. We nourish our bodies and our brains and even our emotional nature, although not always with the best possible food. But when it comes to spiritual nourishment, we starve ourselves.

Spiritual nourishment does not merely mean to read, hear or learn about spiritual truth, or about God and his creation. It does not even mean prayer and meditation, although that's a part. The most important substance of spiritual food is self-development. We have it in our hands to be happy, but we often turn the wrong way.

The same work or effort is not expected of everyone, for each of our tasks and levels of development are different. But anyone reading these words has sufficient means to acquire this food. The Guide suggests that 30 minutes a day is all that's needed for doing the work of spiritual development.

Facing the Music | Negativity

When we only have a vague sense of our negativity, dimly sensing the hurt that we are inflicting on others, we end up hooking others who have their own unconscious conflicts. We go on to blame and punish them for our own lack of love, using their shortcomings as our excuse. Then we build cases against them.

Building a case against another is always a clear indication that we are in our Lower Self. But when we admit our negative intentionality, we set the other free and perform the most fundamental act of love. Honesty, in fact, is the most rare form of love among people.

Without honesty, we stay stuck in the illusion that we are separate, that it's "me *versus* the other" instead of "me *and* the other," and that we need to maintain a strategy to win. Whether we admit our negativity directly to the person or to a healer or therapist who is not personally involved, it is still an act of love toward the universe.

Being imperfect is the human condition. Yet it can be quite humbling to look at parts of ourselves that aren't very pretty. So this journey is not about claiming moral high ground. In fact, the Lower Self doesn't respond well to a moralizing attitude.

Spiritual laws have been created with God's grace so that each choice that takes us away from God eventually causes pain. Pain then becomes the medicine as well as the roadmap that helps us find our way back home.

The Guide says humans think that pain is the worst thing in the world. But we're wrong. The worst thing is being numb. Amazing acts of cruelty can be perpetrated when one is numb.

We each have myriad ways that we distract ourselves from knowing and feeling what is really going on inside. We are semi-aware of the belief that the worst in us is who we really are. And we believe we are alone in our misery and pain. At some point, we realize it's time to stop running.

Learn more in *Doing the Work: Healing Our Body, Mind & Spirit by Getting to Know the Self.*

It is a spiritual law that we can't cheat life. So if we have spent our lives avoiding the feeling of pain, we are—sooner or later—going to have to face that music. The good news is that the pain we fear feeling is not nearly as bad as our fear of it. In other words, the fear of the pain is infinitely worse than the pain itself.

It is also a spiritual law that we can't skip steps. This means that there is no spiritual bypass that will allow us to transcend the work of painstakingly discovering what we really think and believe.

"What you are thinking and believing is the cause of all that is."
– Byron Katie

It is actually a deeply freeing realization to discover that we are responsible—in some way we may not yet understand—for our pain. Once we take responsibility, that means there is a way out. It is possible to set ourselves free.

This work we do to see ourselves and others as we really are builds self-respect. This also leads to a real tolerance and real acceptance of others. This is not a "mask of tolerance" based on not seeing another. Rather, it comes when a person clearly sees another's faults or differences and does not love or respect them any less because of them.

Learn more in *Bones*, Chapter 19: The Giant Misunderstanding About Freedom and Self-Responsibility.

Spiritual Laws*

Law of Brotherhood | "To be able to open your heart to another brings spiritual help that you could not receive by yourself."
– Pathwork Lecture #26

Law of Cause and Effect | "Every act has its consequences."
– Pathwork Lecture #245

Law of Justice | "Love your brother as yourself."
– Pathwork Lecture #30

Law of Karma (Law of Cause and Effect over many Lifetimes) | "Every entity is always given a chance to solve his problems, conflicts and disharmonies in the easiest circumstances possible."
– Pathwork Lecture #38

Law of Living in Truth | "To face life's reality means to face yourself as you are, with all your imperfections. Embrace life whole-heartedly, without fear, without self-pity or being afraid of being hurt. Say to yourself, 'In order to become what I would like to be, I must first, without fear of shame or vanity, face what is in me.' "
– Pathwork Lecture #25

Law of Paying the Price | "There is a price to be paid for everything. He who tries to avoid this will finally pay much dearer."
– Pathwork Lecture #25

Law of Self-Responsibility | "You create your own reality."
– Pathwork Lecture #40

Spiritual Concepts*

Concept of Abundance | "We possess all the powers, faculties and resources to create and bring about what we wish for. It is only our misconceptions and fear of happiness which prevent us from having it." – Pathwork Lecture #157

Concept of Awareness | "You cannot purify—eliminate a problem—if you don't first become aware of it."—Pathwork Lecture #41

Concept of Free Will | "Every individual has complete free will. God has created perfect laws and perfect conditions that his children have the opportunity to follow freely or not."—Pathwork Lecture #18

Concept of Growth | "The only thing that gives meaning to life is to continuously grow."—Pathwork Lecture #89

Concept of Harmony | "A human being living in complete and utter harmony with the life force would not die. Wherever the life force has not been violated, happiness, complete harmony and peace would be yours."—Pathwork Lecture #48

Concept of Sacrifice | "You have to give up what you want to gain." – Pathwork Lecture #17

Concept of Self-Acceptance | "You do not have to be perfect in order to respect yourself. All you have to do is to have a realistic attitude about your imperfections and to adopt a constructive attitude about them."—Pathwork Lecture #31

*Compiled by Matthew Connors, Kirtee Faye, Michael Morgan, Mef Ford and Peter Sampson in 1978.

Learn more in *Spiritual Laws: Hard & Fast Logic for Forging Ahead.*

Giving It Up | Negative Intention

T he idea that we are made in the image of God expresses the reality that like God, we have free will to create. As creators, we can use our intentionality to mold our life forces however we want. But if we have a negative intention to not give and not give in, our energy—which could have been used for creative purposes—gets channeled into destructive patterns that keep us stuck in what the Guide calls vicious circles.

All of our distortions and blindnesses create vicious circles. One primary vicious circle lives in everyone, hidden. There are also many other individual vicious circles. They begin in childhood, where all images are formed. In order to dissolve them, we need to uncover the entire vicious circle. We start by finding an off-ramp, or a way out.

An example of a vicious circle might be: I want love, I don't get it 100% perfectly due to the other's imperfections, I cover up feeling hurt, I judge, I reject, I am lonely and isolated, I want love, repeat. Underneath this is perhaps the belief, "I'm not enough and I'll never be enough."

It may seem that the only options are to go into judgment—which supports the pride of feeling better than—or feel the pain of the rejected inner child—and die to the pain of this illusion. So we keep judging the other—to avoid feeling affected—or possibly collapse into worthlessness

124

and judge the self.

What the undistorted Lower Self energy is really wanting to say is, "I have a need!" Instead the Lower Self says, "I will use the demand that you show up the way I want to justify staying in separation." Its intention is to not take self-responsibility. We need to heal this wound to see the divine longing that is behind this negativity.

There is a basic misconception here that it is not OK to have needs. Staying in deprivation creates acute pain, confirming the belief that "I can't have it." Such misconceptions are used by the Lower Self to justify its demands.

Learn more in *Gems*, Chapter 13: Landing our Desires by Letting Go of Our Demands.

Based on early childhood experiences, the energy has gotten attached to a push-pull dynamic that can never be satisfied: "I reject what I want—love—because it hurts the way I get it." We either make the other wrong, or we are wrong. Pride says, "I need to make the other wrong."

Fear says, "I'm afraid they will hurt me." Self-will says, "I choose to stay isolated to protect my vulnerability." Note that statements coming from the mask, such as, "It's not safe to be in relationship," are an effect, not a cause, and are not at the level of negative intention.

If we cannot find a way out, it is because of our own choice—our negative intention—to stay stuck. It is both a defense and a way to punish others: "I don't like it so I want to punish you." It is a way of not giving anything and demanding everything. Our withholding of love, even if it is due to fear, is as hurtful as active cruelty.

In emotional maturity, we would be able to give and receive love, even if not perfectly, and get our needs met. Instead, negative creations are now being perpetuated in which there is a demand for 100% perfect love, which does not exist on the earth plane.

If we have a problem that we can't seem to solve, there is likely a negative intention that is still hidden. Negative intention in one area seeps across many areas. But we will not find a way out if we play a game of helplessness, dependency and victimization. Self-responsibility is the way to find new solutions.

To heal negative intention, we need to give. Off-ramps for this example include: recognizing the anger of an emotional reaction; feeling the feelings under the anger; speaking one's truth about feeling hurt; being curious about the other; having compassion for the other; accepting that others aren't perfect.

People in addiction recovery programs are often encouraged to "get outside themselves," which means to find a way to give of themselves. For some, this means working with others, for others it means making the coffee. The important thing is to give from the center of ourselves.

This breaks a person out of their inward facing orientation. By re-orienting ourselves to giving, doors also open for receiving—because giving and receiving are one. This lets in the possibility to receive the respect, affection, appreciation—in short, love—the soul longs for.

Learn more in *Bones*, Chapter 17: Overcoming Our Negative Intention by Identifying with Our Spiritual Self.

We work with our withholding by going into the resistance that is held in the body and in the breath. We will first expose the anger that was a protective device saying, "No, this is not what I want!" Under that will be the pain of not receiving perfect love. We must use self-responsibility to ferret out our intention: "What makes me say No?"

We need to re-educate the inner child to realize that, as in the example given, he or she is enough and there is nothing wrong with having a need. We can then use visualization to plant the seed of truth that fulfillment of our longing is possible. And finally, we accept the reality that sometimes the other is going to be able to love us, and sometimes they're not.

The key to life is to find and align with God's will. To do that, we must find our own will—our own positive intention. And that takes commitment. Anything less than 100% commitment will not give us the results we want. Half-measures avail us nothing.

We need a holistic approach, combining our thinking abilities, our intuition and meditation. It won't work to just do the right thing if our motivation is wrong. We will end up still feeling like we're a persecuted victim in a haphazard world.

If, after much work, a vicious circle will still not dissolve, the solution may be found in looking at opposites. For example, if we struggle with a great amount of fear, it may be good to look at how we actually desire to make others afraid of us.

Learn more in *After the Ego*, Chapter 8: Commitment: Cause and Effect.

Immature Attempt to Get Love	Mature Way to Get Love
Person demands love. • Unwilling to give it.	Person wants love and is willing to give it.
Uses a Forcing Current. • Overt and covert control.	No fixed ideas about how it should look.
Other cannot give love due to Forcing Current and their own issues.	Flexible
Person feels slighted.	Disappointments don't kill us.
Hostility and aggression are hidden behind withdrawal, attack or submission.	No hidden hostility.
Other perceives hostility and reacts.	No resentments.
Bleakness	Other feels openness and spontaneous flow.
Escape to fantasy and imagined situation of getting approval, love.	Get love and give love.
Want instant gratification.	
Dramatize, build cases against the other, seek sympathy.	
Feel disappointment.	
Demand love.	

The Primary Vicious Circle

1. Have inferiority feelings due to artificially high standards.
2. Demand to be loved/admired. "I have failed. I am inferior. If I could receive great love/respect/admiration, it will prove I am not worthless."
3. Duality: Perfect love exists; if I didn't get it, my parents were wrong.
4. Craving for love becomes immature: the child wants love from everyone, but has no intention of loving.
5. Feeling of rejection causes hatred, resentment, hostility and aggression toward the ones the child love most.
6. This conflict in the psyche causes shame.
7. Shame is pushed into the unconscious.
8. Hate for parents creates guilt, which becomes the source of conflict for the adult.
9. Guilt creates desire to be punished.
10. Unconscious fear of punishment arises.
11. This shortcuts feelings of happiness and pleasure; we feel undeserving.
12. The child fears that if these good things happen, the punishment will be greater.
13. The child unconsciously avoids happiness by creating situations and patterns that destroy everything most dearly wished for.
14. Duality: Yearn for happiness; fear happiness.
15. The stronger one desires happiness, the guiltier one feels.
16. Images are gathered which fortify this vicious circle.
17. Fear of punishment from others is great. Unconsciously decide to punish self to avoid humiliation, helplessness, degradation.
18. Self-punishments include physical disease, mishaps, difficulties, failures and conflicts, depending on images.

Split | Desire not to be punished; bargain to be best at everything to atone for past hate.

Truth | No one needs to be punished. We are lovable as we are.

Breaking the Mold | The No-Current

If human consciousness is the sculptor, our soul substance is the material it molds. It contains our conscious Yes, which is based on truthful insight and breeds love and unity. It also contains our unconscious No, which is destructive and breeds hate and disunity. Where there is unfulfillment or a feeling of being unlucky, both a Yes and a No must be present. This is like driving with the brakes on.

If a No-current is driven underground, the Yes becomes frantic, creating tension and pressure. This convinces us of the "rightness" of our desire for fulfillment but is really our clue we need to search for the root cause of our unfulfillment. Even if we discover our hidden fears, this rarely changes things because there is still a hidden No-current.

The work is to uncover the No, understand the faulty premise, and shed the old belief. When we find the statement of our actual unconscious belief, we will see how we actually cringe from fulfillment. For example, if a child received painful experiences as part of the imperfect love it was given, the child may have internalized the push-pull dynamic of rejecting the one it wants to love. The belief may then be "I need to have someone I reject."

No's are connected with an original image that was already molded into the soul substance when a person was born. It is not that we are hard-wired this way and cannot change. Rather, healing these deep soul dents is the reason for this incarnation. The Guide teaches that they typically do not originate in this lifetime. If they do, they will be easy to resolve once the adult reasoning mind considers the reality of the situation.

We weaken the No-current by allowing the Yes-current to observe it: "I now say Yes to wanting to understand the No. I take the reins in my hands." We can start by examining the layers that are accessible. The half-conscious materials to work with are emotional reactions and fantasies. We must see how we say No.

- Where am I dissatisfied?
- What would I want to be different?
- Is there something in me that does not want it or fears it?
- How do I detect this in my daily life?

Positive thinking and affirmations create a temporary hopefulness and even some success. But to truly change a No-current requires that, in Jesus' words, we must be "reborn." Dissolving a No that is being held by the will is like turning a battleship. We need to go slow.

We must get quiet and call on divine strength to help us see the truth and to have the stamina to change. When sitting in emptiness, we will first see the destructive elements floating up. Then we will be able to tap the constructive elements hidden deep within. Note that some Yes-currents, such as greed, are really products of a No-current.

Just knowing about a No-current will not stop it. We need to observe it in action daily to see and feel its effect, and to see why change is desirable. The final decisive factor is us. We need to change the "I can't" to "it is possible." This will eliminate the cringing, the fantasies and the frantic Yes. By using our will and positive intention to change, only we can end our suffering. After this, we can never be the same. We will see the truth of divine order.

Learn more in *Bones*, Chapter 15: Learning to Speak the Language of the Unconscious.

Steps for Purifying and Transforming the Lower Self*

1. Have desire to work with Lower Self to transform it.
2. Have desire to know what else we are, knowing we are more than we thought we were.
3. Establish contact with the divine and ask for help in having the strength, stamina and ability to change.
4. Use thought processes in a new way: change "I can't" to "it is possible."
5. Be willing to feel original pain, and also the present pain of how this has been affecting our life.
6. Meditate on wanting to go in and see what we have been avoiding.
7. Be willing to see the No-currents.
8. Compare the parts of our life where we are fulfilled with those areas where we are not. Feel the difference.
9. Talk out our problem.
10. Meditate: "The truth cannot harm me, although something ignorant in me rebels against it. In spite of it, I say Yes. I take the reins into my own hands."
11. Observe negative attitudes.
    a. Question feelings and reactions to negative creations.
    b. Work through effect on self and others—what price do we pay?
    c. See the falsity of pretenses, looking underneath blame and victimization. "What I do doesn't work, this is why not, and I wish to operate in a different way." More insight will lead to more will to give it up.
12. Shift identification to the observer.
13. Find the essence of the quality that is negative.
14. Shift identity and attitude by asking: "What attitude do I choose toward what I now observe in me and do not like?" See what our choices are as we observe the destructive attitudes and intentions within.
15. Meditate with three voices: Conscious mind with the Lower Self (the inner child); conscious mind with the Higher Self; Higher Self with the inner child.

16. Say the Gateway Prayer.
17. Recognize the Stages of Awareness:
    a. Half-asleep climate—do not know who we are and blindly battle against what we hate about ourselves.
    b. Observe, acknowledge, and articulate what we do not like.
    c. Become aware that the "I," or real self which observes, can make new decisions and choices.
    d. Comprehend the previously hated aspects, which means their dissolution and integration.
18. Have a conscious inner dialogue as we uncover the unconscious:
    a. Admit what we uncover.
    b. Know why attitudes are negative and how they distort truth.
    c. Intelligently consider the situation versus the child's view. Bring reason to emotions.
    d. Express the irrational desire behind the destructive attitude.
        i. How does it oppose reality, fairness, truth?
        ii. Why is it wrong? How could it be different?
19. Visualize the state we want to grow into.

* Created by Cynthia Schwartzberg.

Learn more in *Gems*, Chapter 14: How to Visualize Living in a State of Unity, in *Finding Gold*, Chapter 12: Approach to Self: Self-Forgiveness Without Condoning the Lower Self, and in *Pearls*, Chapter 14: Meditating to Connect Three Voices: The Ego, the Lower Self & the Higher Self.

Aligning with Longing | Needs

E very child has real needs—for good feelings, attention, affection and appreciation of its uniqueness. Every child also has an unrealistic desire to be loved, cared for and accepted 100%. But since parents are humans with faults of their own, they cannot always give love maturely, and certainly cannot give 100% devotion as the child desires.

So in every little life, there will be the pain of having unmet needs. This pain will be experienced as anger toward the ones the child loves most, which often results in feelings of guilt. When this pain is resisted, these unfelt feelings become stuck in our beings and in our bodies.

Then, as a person grows older, these once-real-needs turn into false needs. Because what was a real need for the child is no longer a real need for the adult. A mature adult is capable of tolerating frustration, of delaying gratification, and of having genuine good feelings, even if they are not liked by everyone.

For the immature adult, these false needs become demands: to always be loved, never be hurt, and have others be responsible for us and our feelings of well-being. But for the adult, getting fulfillment this way is simply not possible. Even if it came to us, it could not provide the happiness we long for, because this is now an inside job. We must come to see that we are the one who can now fulfill our needs.

This resulting lack of gratification leads to the pain of frustration, which in an immature state, cannot be tolerated. Worse yet, this combination of lack of gratification and frustration seems to confirm that we were wrong to even have needs.

We then defend against this pain, using habitual, unconscious strategies that actually cause us to act contrary to our best interest and end up starving the now-buried-real-needs even more.

With part of us disapproving of even having needs, we repress our needs further. This saying No to our real needs is a blindness that disconnects us from ourselves. The result is a feeling of urgency. Urgency is always a blinking light that there is something unconscious that needs to be surfaced. But instead, we often mistake urgency for "proof" of how much we want what we want—which is often to receive 100% love and to be cared for by another.

Our inability to let go of our demand for fulfillment of false needs—to relinquish fulfillment *temporarily*—creates self-contempt, as we are not able to tolerate the frustration of "not having." As such, we cannot love and accept ourselves, which leads to lack of self-confidence along with more demand for fulfillment from others.

And we are back where we started, but more lost in a maze of confusion, demands, buried longings and unmet needs.

The good news is that there is a way out. It is through the doorway of awareness. At first it will happen only in hindsight, and slowly we will come to see this vicious circle playing out in the moment. And that is when we have the opportunity to make another choice.

If we have not fully experienced our past, we must attract similar experiences later in life. So then, when a hurt, criticism or frustration arises, we need to become aware of the strong reaction taking place in ourselves, and become willing to express the unexperienced residual feelings.

It can also help to bring reason to our emotions by asking ourselves: Is it true that I must perish because I have endured pain? How much am I really hurt by this experience that I believe hurts me?

Real, Healthy Adult Needs

- Harmony
- Sexual Pleasure
- Self-Assertion
- Independence
- Success
- Happiness
- Fulfillment
- Self-Confidence
- Self-Respect
- Self-Expression
- Spiritual Growth
- Companionship
- Love

We need to see how our misconceptions about life color our perceptions about others, and contribute to the way we show up in life, making demands on others that can never be fulfilled:

- Always needing to be loved and accepted.
- Never being hurt.
- Being dependent on others for good feelings.

To experience fulfillment of our real needs, there must be a conscious Yes to less-than-perfect fulfillment. We need to come into reality, seeing that actual fulfillment is not perfect, but it is better than childish fantasy. We will see that both giving love and receiving love are two sides of the same coin, and that one cannot survive without the other.

We must also learn to relinquish—to be able to wait, to give something up *for now*—and to be able to tolerate that frustration. Being able to do this creates strength, self-confidence and healthy self-respect, all of which are signs of maturity. These are needed to give up false needs.

As children, we are dependent on our parents. But as we mature, we need to learn to stand on our own. Otherwise we grow up but remain emotionally dependent on something or someone other than oneself, which creates self-alienation. In truth, our ability to experience pleasure and peace does not depend on others.

It is denial of our original pain that creates suffering. Anxiety disappears when we look within for the cause of suffering. This is what it means to take on self-responsibility.

"Do not abandon the longing that comes from the sense that your life could be much more, that you could live without painful tortured confusions, and function on a level of inner resilience, contentment and security.

It is a state of experiencing and expressing deep feelings and blissful pleasure, where you are capable of meeting life without fear because you no longer fear yourself."

– Pathwork Lecture #204

Humor is a divine quality that fulfills our need for pleasure. Sometimes, however, it gets distorted into sarcasm, cynicism, or in certain ways, irony, using humor as a defense. It is a way to rebel and express the violence and rage in us, giving it a modified outlet. It is as though a tremendous power is only allowed to trickle out in a very ineffective way. But this can put us in a greater problem with the world.

In this remembrance of Eva, included in a small tribute booklet printed after her death in 1979, someone close to her offered this humorous little anecdote, joyfully sharing his light after hers went out:

It is a privilege to have known Eva for twenty-one years, to be so long on the path, and to have had so many conversations with Eva and the Guide. When I met Eva, I was having breakdowns and was possessed by a spirit. The Guide told me how to exorcize the demons.

Before sessions, Eva would dial her own number so that the session would not be interrupted by telephone calls, and then she would put the telephone under a pillow.

One day, I sat down and the Guide started talking to me. Then, I felt a sensation in my ass and I said to the Guide, "Excuse me, but when the spirits speak, they usually come in through my back. This time they come in through my ass. What can I do?"

So the Guide said to me, "My dear son, I assure you that's not possible, that a spirit could come in through there." And he told me, "Before you get alarmed, figure out what it is." He said to me, "Please look around you for what it is."

So I looked under the pillow and found the telephone.

– Jose Asencio

Holding It In | The Body

W hen something painful happens in childhood, we deny our feelings. This stops the flow of life force, stagnating energy and creating places of frozen energy in the body. All bodies have a typical way of defending or armoring themselves against these painful early-childhood feelings. So our bodies can show us the main issues we are carrying for transformation.

In the mid-1960s, Eva met and later married Dr. John Pierrakos, a psychiatrist and co-creator of a school of therapy known as bio-energetics. The teachings from the Guide helped transform his work in bio-energetics into Core Energetics, which developed the teachings about character structures.

They are a tool we can use to read the body's messages about a person's needs for love that have not been met. When the body is fully seen and accepted, a deeper level of healing happens. This information should not be used as ammunition for criticism.

Each of the five character structures, or body types, reflects a pattern of frozen emotions and rigidified thinking, or images, typical of arrested development, or trauma, at each of the five primary developmental stages. Following is a very brief overview of the physical and emotional attributes of each:*

Character Structures

Schizoid
Age of Wounding
- Before birth or early infancy.

Trauma
- Hostile/rejecting mother; Unwanted and doesn't want to be here.

Physical/Energetic Patterns
- Energy gives out easily; Elongated, disjointed, ungrounded; Left-right asymmetry.

Life's Work
- Pull one's life together; Join the pieces; Organize and fully manifest creative and spiritual core qualities; Surrender to being a human.

Oral
Age of Wounding
- During breast feeding period; Early childhood.

Trauma
- Abandonment; Deprivation

Physical/Energetic Patterns
- Tires easily, headaches; Undercharged, thin, elongated body; Chest collapsed; Slumped shoulders; Fallen arches; Undercharged legs; Not muscular.

Life's Work
- Stand on one's own two feet; Learn to nourish self and give to others.

Masochist
Age of Wounding
- Autonomy stage (age 2).

Trauma
- Smothering mother; Forced feeding and evacuation; Humiliated and shamed about bodily functions; Little attention to emotional or spiritual needs; Independent self-expression blocked.

Physical/Energetic Patterns

- Energy stagnant, held; Earth-bound; Muscle-bound; Heavy set; Rounded back, heavy shoulders.

Life's Work

- Develop creative self-expression.

Psychopath

Age of Wounding

- Early individuation (ages 1-2), age of natural narcissism; Later (ages 3-4) if seduction by parent has sexual aspect.

Trauma

- Seduction-betrayal; Seductive parent results in child choosing specialness over real needs, feelings, sexuality.

Physical/Energetic Patterns

- Energy in upper body, with especially strong charge in head; Big shoulders, narrow waist or hips; In women, may reverse to weight in pelvis and thighs; Ungrounded, unbalanced.

Life's Work

- Feel self as part of humanity, releasing the specialness that sets one apart from others.

Rigid

Age of Wounding

- Genital stage (ages 4-5); Strong re-emergence of conflict at puberty.

Trauma

- Sexual rejection results in splitting of sexuality and heart feelings.

Physical/Energetic Patterns

- High energy; Integrated, harmonious body; Intellect and will active; Strong boundaries; Heart is defended.

Life's Work

- Bring feeling and compassion into life activities; Connect heart and sexuality in romantic relationship.

Introduction to Core Energetics; Susan Thesenga, April 1998.

Everyone contains aspects of each structure because we all experience many of the same hurts. The fragmenting from pain is more heavily pronounced in the Schizoid, but everyone has split off child aspects. The nonfulfillment of needs that the Oral is most impacted by, is also common to us all.

The withholding due to our negative intention, which shows up strongly for the Masochist, is a universal Lower Self response. And the push-pull dynamic from rejecting the one we love shows up in the Psychopathic dance with seduction and betrayal, and the Rigid's struggle to open their heart when their sexuality is turned on.

That said, most people's bodies more strongly reflect the characteristics of one or two of the structures, depending on the age at which the most wounding—and therefore defending—occurred.

What these body types are revealing are the distortions. If we look a bit deeper, we can see the essence each one is holding. We want to hold a space for who we really are, having compassion especially as we go into dark places. The question we are always asking is, "What are we hiding?" A big belly may be hiding creativity. Collapsed shoulders may hide a tender heart.

Essence Beneath the Body Armor

Schizoid | Spiritual connection, intuitive.

Oral | Intelligent (strong mind, articulate), sensitive, empathetic.

Masochist | Big heart, giving; creative, fun-loving; persistent, hard working.

Psychopath | Courage, love, leadership.

Rigid | Passion, leadership, commitment, clarity, endurance.

We can also look at how our body structures relate to our primary essence or Personality Type:

Reason Type | Experienced loneliness, rejection: *Schizoid, Rigid*

Emotion Type | Experienced abandonment, lack of touch: *Oral*

Will Type | Experienced mastery of things due to wounding in later development: *Masochist, Psychopathic*

We know that when an event happens, people interpret it differently based on their own stuck energy. This explains why siblings often have differing responses to the same parent. When we don't feel our feelings, we carry this waste into the next life.

We also know this stuck energy manifests as illness in our bodies. Without movement, life does not exist. Muscles, for example, atrophy quickly without movement. Health issues in our bodies then are an effect, and not a cause. Answers from the Guide revealing the deeper origin of specific health concerns can be found under the topic Body & Health on *The Guide Speaks*.

Healing is all about freeing up stuck energy and returning to our original divine self, which is love. But the Guide teaches that in intimate relationships, the love force can't grow when separated from sex and eros. This bumps up against society's taboos about the erotic sexual force, and has lead to over-development of intellectual areas instead of nurturing our ability to learn to love.

Distorted sexual feelings—which were only distorted because they were denied—must be faced to change. They are often hidden under hostility, which is hard to face because it contradicts the Idealized Self Image. Indeed, hostility is often more accepted in a family than pleasure, so pleasurable feelings are often buried deepest. We must unfold all of these layers.

As babies, all experiences are physical because there has been no mental or emotional development yet. So everything that happens in a person's life will be recorded, so to speak, in the memory tracks of the physical body. This includes the attachment of the pleasure drive to painful experience.

Our adult sexual experiences will then show us the way in which energy was first blocked. Because due to this cross-wiring, in order for the life force to be pleasurably activated during sex, the destructiveness must be re-experienced. Therefore the original conflict—as well as the resolution—shows up in sexual fantasies, which are needed for sexual pleasure and release. Approaching healing by looking through the lens of sexual fantasies is an efficient way to uncover our deepest wounds. It is also very sensitive and sacred work.

Learn more in *The Pull*, Chapter 5: Pleasure: The Full Pulsation of Life, Chapter 6: The Forces of Love, Eros and Sex, and Chapter 7: The Spiritual Symbolism and Significance of Sexuality; and in *Doing the Work*, Chapter 12: TAKING THE LONG WAY HOME | Doing the Work.

Bucking the Burden | Guilt

B ecause our drive for pleasure gets attached to destructiveness, we experience guilt due to the ways we inflict pain on others. But if we can't
feel the pain of what others did to us, we can't feel the pain of our guilt for
what we do to others. We need to open to feeling the pain caused by our withholding, spite and maligning. That is, we need to have genuine remorse for the
pain we cause and not get lost in false guilt.

It may help to understand the difference between guilt and remorse.
When we feel guilt, we are in effect saying, "I'm beyond redemption and
deserve to feel devastated." We feel this way because we believe that our
Lower Self is all of us. We need to be aware of this powerful and dangerous
wrong thinking. It's not true and it's an insult to God and all of creation, of
which we—including our Higher Self—are an integral part.

Our self-devastating guilt is also integrally linked with our distrust of life.
Our guilt causes us to cut ourselves off from the flow of divinity by going
immediately to whitewashing our faults and failings—which of course are
the areas we need to be facing and honestly owning.

With remorse, we are simply recognizing where we fall short—our faults
and impurities, our shortcomings and limitations—admitting that there are
parts of us that violate spiritual law. We feel regret and are willing to admit
the truth about our destructiveness, recognizing that it's a useless waste of
energy and hurts others and ourselves. We sincerely want to change. With

remorse, our self-confrontation is completely different from self-devastating guilt.

If we feel remorseful, it is possible to say, "It's true that I have this or that shortcoming or fault—I'm petty or dishonest, I have false pride or hatred or whatever—but this isn't all of who I am. The part of me that recognizes, regrets and wants to change is aligned with my divine self—my Higher Self—which ultimately will overcome whatever I feel remorseful about." In this case, the "I" that can dislike aspects of ourselves and wants to change those destructive, untruthful, deviating aspects doesn't fall apart, even as it notices that something needs to be healed.

Guilt involves a lack of faith in All That Is. Remorse is an emotion that will carry us home, feeling the sadness of the effects of our Lower Self and motivating us to discover the true source of all life.

Guilt also arises from a distortion of our urge for self-realization. In our competitiveness, we try to measure what cannot be measured: one person versus another. Our push for specialness comes from this belief that we can—and need to—triumph over others.

We need to learn to see the truth about limitless abundance—that our individuality is never in conflict with anyone else. We can assert ourselves without being cruel or depriving others. We can give up our immediate advantage for the sake of others. We can say Yes to ourselves without saying No to others. Love and self-exertion can co-exist. Giving fulfillment to ourselves allows us to give to others. After all, we can't give what we don't have.

Setting the Sails | Symbols

S igns and symbols are a gift from God to help us navigate our journey. In the first lecture, the Guide used an analogy in which all of life is the sea, and each individual life is a boat. This symbolism captures the stormy aspects of life and the calm waters that allow time to regroup in between storms. The storms are always followed by sunshine, and the sun in fact is always present behind the clouds. The journey alternates between storms and calm until our boat arrives at its destination, which is the firm land of the Spirit World—our true home.

If we are skilled captains and not afraid of danger, we will direct our boat wisely through the elements, gathering strength during the smooth periods to be ready for the next storm. Another of us might get nervous and lose inner control when a storm is brewing. Yet another may be so scared that in extreme fear, no effort is made to steer the boat at all and it drifts through storms, not gaining anything.

The clouds and storms are the tests that life brings to each of us. If we reach out to God and ask for help, we can be given more strength to steer our little boat well, even through storms. The journey all depends on how well we direct our life.

Learn more in *Gems*, Chapter 16: Relaxing into the Struggle to Find the Oneness.

In the final lecture, the Guide once again spoke of the beautiful symbolism of the sea, pointing out how it tells us loudly and clearly that nothing is ever lost. We can observe this in the ebb and flow of the water. When it recedes, it seems to disappear and no longer exist. Of course, it continues to exist in the greater pool and it will return. Individual consciousness is the same.

In the ebb and the flow, we also see a certain rhythm. In life, we too often allow our disruptive minds to become insensitive to our own unique rhythm patterns, which we need to learn to be in harmony with.

When we seek connections between our outer world and our insides and the answers fail to come, we may be out of rhythm. The waiting time can then be used to find qualities in ourselves that we can only see in times of ebb, never flow. It's like having a chance to look closely at the whalebones and seashells lying on the sand, which we can't get to once the tide comes back in. Just as the time span between high tide and low tide is never exactly the same, in the same way, we need to sense our own rhythm in all things.

The Guide tells us that we will recognize this type of symbolism more as we awaken. Then we will come to view the universe in a whole new way. We will see that everything has purpose, nothing is for naught, and there is a magnificent plan at work to bring us all to Oneness.

We will one day find that instead of being the holder of light, we will no longer need the light. Because we will become what we've always been—the illuminating urge itself.

"The world then goes about its business. Its business is light that no darkness opposes because it does not illuminate something, but is the illuminating urge itself."

– Two steps in the *Magi Process*, by Jason Shulman

Hitting the Road | Next Steps

With lectures given every month for over twenty years, the body of material that comprises these teachings is extensive. Over the years, the Guide offered several lectures to help summarize what this work is about.

#25 The Path: Initial Steps, Preparation and Decisions
#193 Resume of the Basic Principles of the Pathwork: Its Aims and Process
#204 What is the Path?

If we feel ready to delve further into these teachings, we can trust our own guidance about which lectures or Q&As to read next. Avoid the temptation to satisfy the ego's thirst for knowledge if it wants to read everything before doing anything. We could liken that to a thirsty person trying to drink from a fire hose, unable to get the few cups of water really needed right now. A garden hose would be a wiser choice.

Also know that little may actually change in our life if we only read this material. Some openings will surely happen and shifts may occur. But we must apply these teachings to the everyday happenings in our lives to really make progress.

If we are ready to do this work, we will be guided to someone who can help us. We can pray to align with our Higher Self—the part that wants to heal. This is our true Godself and it is worth searching for.

"Two birds were sitting on a wire. One made a decision to fly south for the winter. Now how many birds are sitting on the wire? Two. The one only made a decision."
– Shared by someone anonymously at an AA meeting

The road we are on is a long one with many twists and turns, which is true whether one follows a spiritual path such as this or not. This path the Guide is leading us on is particularly narrow in the way it calls for rigorous self-honesty. But by following it we can accomplish in one lifetime what might otherwise take twenty.

It is a long journey. But God's laws have been created so that eventually all will arrive once again in God's loving embrace. We have all the time in the world. But how much time do we really want to take?

From *Proverbs and Tiny Songs*

II

  Why should we call
these accidental furrows roads?...
Everyone who moves on walks
like Jesus, on the sea.

VI

  You walking, your footsteps *are*
the road, and nothing else;
there is no road, walker,
you make the road by walking.
By walking you make the road,
and when you look backward,
you see the path that you
never will step on again.
Walker, there is no road,
Only wind-trails in the sea.

  − By Antonio Machado (1875−1939),
  translated by Robert Bly

About the Author

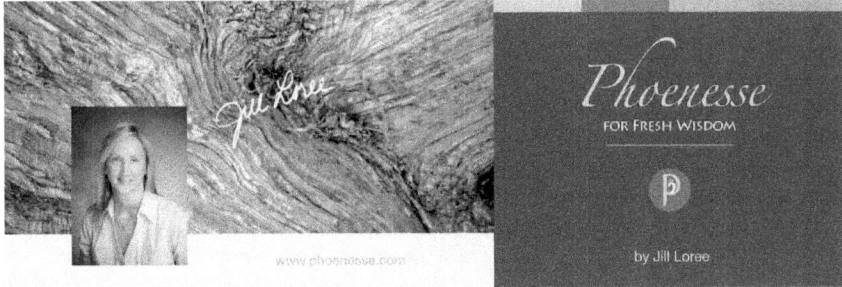

Jill Loree
Founder of Phoenesse

A neatnik with a ready sense of humor, Jill Loree's first job as a root-beer-stand carhop in northern Wisconsin was an early sign that things could only get better.

She would go on to throw pizzas and bartend while in college, before discovering that the sweet spot of her 30-year sales-and-marketing career would be in business-to-business advertising. A true Gemini, she has a degree in chemistry and a flair for writing. Her brain fires on both the left and right sides.

That said, her real passion in life has been her spiritual path. Raised in the Lutheran faith, she became a more deeply spiritual person in the rooms of Alcoholics Anonymous, a spiritual recovery program, starting in 1989. In 1997, she was introduced to the wisdom of the Pathwork, which she describes as "having walked through the doorway of a fourth step and found the whole library."

She completed four years of Pathwork Helpership training in 2007 followed by four years of apprenticing and discernment before stepping into her full Helpership in 2011. She has been a teacher in the Transformation Program offered at Sevenoaks Retreat Center in Madison, Virginia, operated by Mid-Atlantic Pathwork, where she also led marketing activities for over two years and served on the Board of Trustees.

In 2012, Jill completed four years of kabbalah training in a course called the Soul's Journey, achieving certification for hands-on healing using the energies embodied in the tree of life.

Not bad for a former pom-pom squad captain who once played Dolly in *Hello Dolly!* She is now the proud mom of two adult children, Charlie and Jackson, who were born and raised in Atlanta. Jill Loree is delighted to be married to Scott Wisler, but continues to use her middle name as her last (it's pronounced loh-REE). In her spare time she enjoys reading, writing, yoga, golf, skiing and hiking, especially in the mountains.

In 2014, she consciously decoupled from the corporate world and is now dedicating her life to writing and teaching about spirituality, personal healing and self-discovery.

Catch up with Jill at www.phoenesse.com.

phoenesse®
FIND YOUR TRUE YOU.

More from Phoenesse

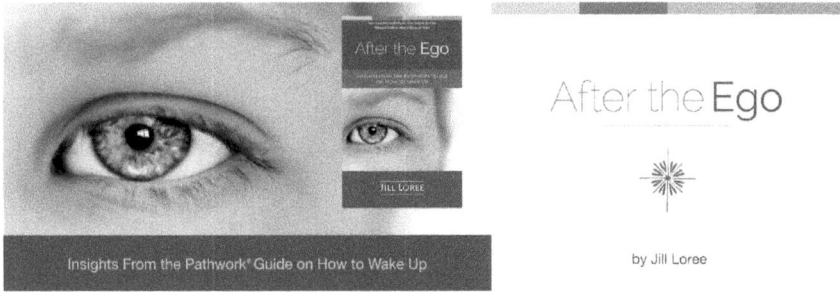

After the Ego

by Jill Loree

AFTER THE EGO
Insights from the Pathwork® Guide on How to Wake Up

Whether or not we lead meaningful and fulfilling lives depends entirely on the relationship between our ego and our Real Self. All these teachings from the Pathwork Guide are pointing to this, prying at it from a multitude of directions to help us open to this truth as our personal experience. For if this relationship is in balance, everything falls nicely into place.

But now, as a new world unfolds from the new consciousness sweeping Earth, many are struggling to find their footing. What every soul on Earth is actually noticing is where they currently stand on their personal journey to find their Real Self and live from this truthful inner space.

After the Ego reveals key facets of the complex and fascinating phenomenon behind the inner "earthquakes" now shaking so many people, and walks us through the vital process of awakening from duality.

Now is the moment for all of us to pay attention—not just to the unprecedented outer events in our world, but to what is happening within.

Now is the time to wake up.

More from Phoenesse

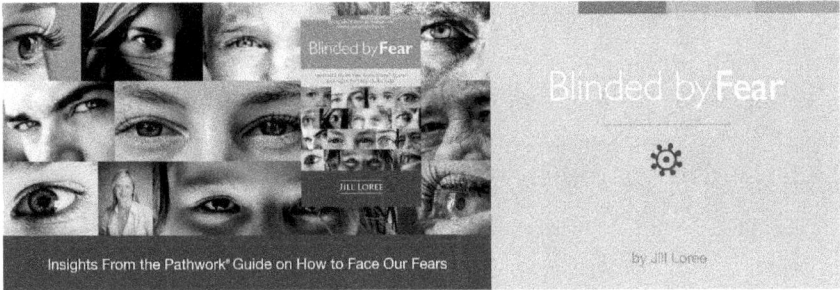

BLINDED BY FEAR
Insights From the Pathwork® Guide on How to Face Our Fears

It's an error to think that becoming aware of our fears—of turning towards them and facing them in the light—will give them more power. Many of us, in fact, mistakenly believe that if we avoid looking at them, they will not overtake us. So we turn a blind eye, hoping to avoid something unpleasant.

In truth, it's not awareness of our fears that causes us problems, but our fearful attitude about even looking at them. By not facing our fears, we keep fighting the parts of ourselves that happen to be in fear, right now. We cramp up our whole being—including our bodies—bracing against our feelings of fear. But if we'll bring our fears into the fresh air of our conscious awareness, they will lose their terrible roar.

In this collection of insights from the Pathwork Guide about facing our fears, fear is illuminated from many perspectives. And once we start to see our fears for what they truly are, we can begin to watch them slip away.

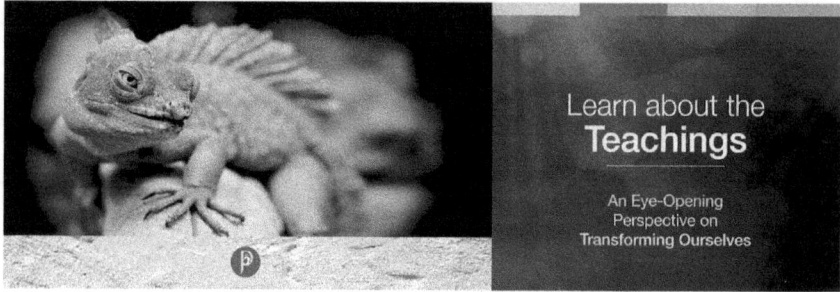

Learn about the
Teachings

An Eye-Opening
Perspective on
Transforming Ourselves

Understand these Spiritual Teachings

Read an overview of the Pathwork Guide's teachings about personal self-development on the Phoenesse website. This profound spiritual wisdom is presented in three parts:

- **The Work of Healing:** Learn about the work of incarnating as a human into this land of duality, and the steps we can take to unwind our difficulties and free ourselves from struggle.
- **The Prequel:** Learn about the series of events that unfolded in the Spirit World, landing us here in this difficult dimension.
- **The Rescue:** Learn what happened when we lost our free will, how we got it back, and who we should thank.

www.phoenesse.com

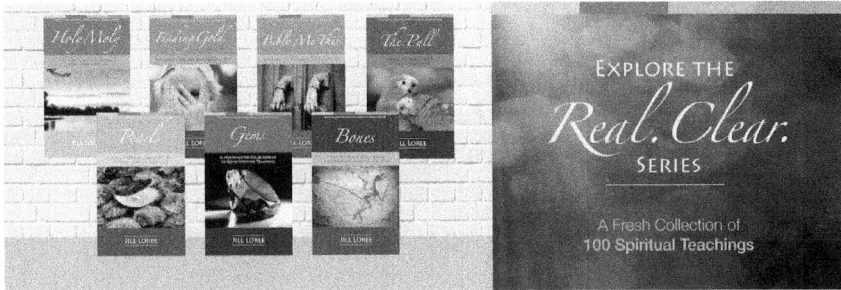

Real.Clear.
A Seven-Book Series of Spiritual Teachings

The *Real.Clear.* series offers a fresh approach to timeless spiritual teachings by way of easier-to-read language; it's the Pathwork Guide's wisdom in Jill Loree's words. Each book is written with a bit of levity because, as Mary Poppins put it, "A spoonful of sugar helps the medicine go down."

HOLY MOLY: The Story of Duality, Darkness and a Daring Rescue

There's one story, as ancient and ageless as anything one can imagine, that lays a foundation on which all other truths stand. It exposes the origin of opposites. It illuminates the reality of darkness in our midst. It speaks of herculean efforts made on our behalf. This is that story.

FINDING GOLD: The Search for Our Own Precious Self

The journey to finding the whole amazing nugget of the Real Self is a lot like prospecting for gold. Both combine the lure of potential and the excitement of seeing a sparkling possibility, with needing to have the patience of a saint.

It helps to have a map of our inner landscape and a headlamp for seeing into dark corners. That's what Jill Loree has created in this collection of spiritual teachings called *Finding Gold*.

BIBLE ME THIS: Releasing the Riddles of Holy Scripture

The Bible is a stumper for many of us, not unlike the Riddler teasing Batman with his "riddle me this" taunts. But what if we could know what some of those obscure passages mean? What's the truth hidden in the myth of Adam & Eve? And what was up with that Tower of Babel?

Bible Me This is a collection of in-depth answers to a variety of questions asked of the Guide about the Bible.

THE PULL: Relationships & Their Spiritual Significance

The Pull is about discovering the truth about relationships: they are the doorway through which we ultimately can come to know ourselves, God and another person; through them, we can learn to fully live. Because while life may be many things, more than anything else, it is all about relationships. *The Pull* walks us through the delicate dance of intimate relationships, helping us navigate one of the most challenging aspects of life.

PEARLS: A Mind-Opening Collection of 17 Fresh Spiritual Teachings

In this classic, practical collection, Jill Loree strings together timeless spiritual teachings, each carefully polished with a light touch. Topics include: Privacy & Secrecy • The Lord's Prayer • Political Systems • The Superstition of Pessimism • Preparing to Reincarnate • Our Relationship to Time • Grace & Deficit • The Power of Words • Perfectionism • Authority • Order • Positive Thinking • Three Faces of Evil • Meditation for Three Voices • The Spiritual Meaning of Crisis • Leadership • Letting Go & Letting God

GEMS: A Multifaceted Collection of 16 Clear Spiritual Teachings

Clear and radiant, colorful and deep, each sparkling gem in this collection of spiritual teachings taken mostly from the final 50 lectures out of nearly 250, offers a ray of light to help illuminate our steps to reaching oneness.

BONES: A Building-Block Collection of 19 Fundamental Spiritual Teachings

This collection is like the bones of a body—a framework around which the remaining body of work can arrange itself. Sure, there's a lot that needs to be filled in to make it all come to life, but with *Bones*, now we've got the basic building blocks in place. Plus the words go down like a strawberry milkshake—pleasing to the tongue yet with all the calcium we need for optimum health.

NUTSHELLS: Short & Sweet Spiritual Insights

Nutshells are short-and-sweet daily spiritual insights carved from three books: *Pearls*, *Gems* and *Bones*. Meaningful inspirations and memorable phrases are woven together to create a new creation that largely resembles the original form. Like the acorn that contains the potential for the oak tree, these nuggets of wisdom hold the power to change our whole perspective on life.

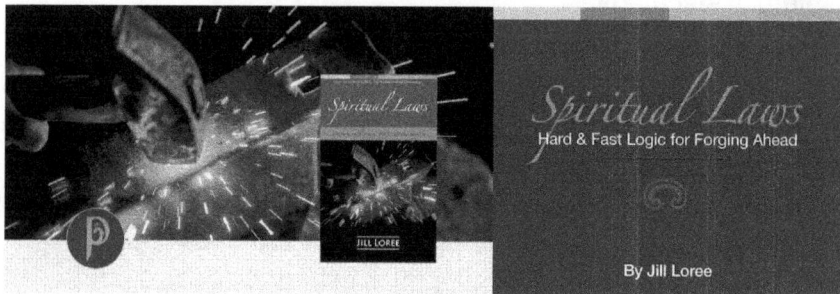

Spiritual Laws
Hard & Fast Logic for Forging Ahead

Just what are the laws that rule this precious land? Turns out, there are an infinite number of laws that govern everything that happens. And while *Spiritual Laws* does not claim to be comprehensive in covering them all, this sampling of teachings from the Pathwork Guide does a nice job of explaining how this sphere works.

Understanding this will help us grasp the truth that behind our trials, there is a method. That someone or something is behind life, working out a plan. So gather round and listen up, because there are important guidelines we could all stand to know more about, and the hammer is about to drop.

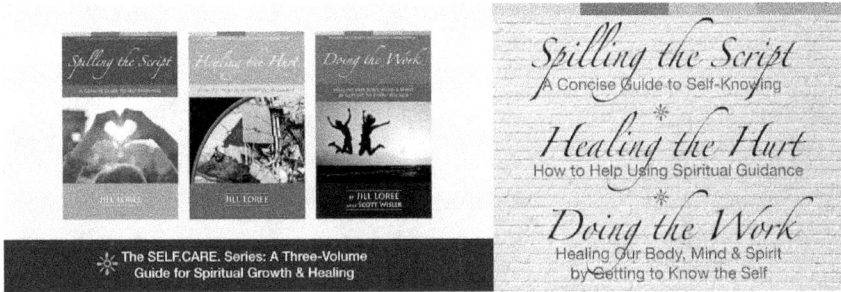

Self.Care.
A Three-Book Teaching Series

The *Self.Care.* How-to-Heal series offers a bird's-eye view of the Pathwork Guide's teachings and shows us how to apply them in working with ourselves and others.

SPILLING THE SCRIPT: A Concise Guide to Self-Knowing

Now, for the first time, powerful spiritual teachings from the Guide are available in one concise book. Jill Loree has written *Spilling the Script* to deliver a clear, high-level perspective about self-discovery and healing, giving us the map we need for following this life-changing path to oneness.

The goal of this spiritual journey is to make contact with our divine core so we can transition from living in duality to discovering the joy of being in unity. For even as we believe ourselves to be victims of an unfair universe, the truth is that we are continually guarding ourselves against pain, and through our defended approach to life we unknowingly bring about our current life circumstances. But we can make new choices.

Bit by bit, as we come out of the trance we have been in, we begin to see cause and effect, and to take responsibility for the state of our lives. Gradually, our lives transform. We once again can sense our essential nature and eternal connectedness with all that is.

"You will find how you cause all your difficulties. You have already stopped regarding these words as mere theory, but the better you progress,

the more will you truly understand just how and why you cause your hard-
ships. By so doing, you gain the key to changing your life."

–Pathwork Guide, Lecture #78

HEALING THE HURT: How to Heal Using Spiritual Guidance

The work of healing our fractured inner selves takes a little finesse, a lot
of stick-to-it-iveness, and the skilled help of someone who has gone down
this road before. Being a Helper then is about applying all we have learned
on our own healing journey to help guide others through the process of re-
unifying their fragmented hidden places.

That may sound simple, but it's surely not easy. It's also not easy to be the
Worker, the one who does this work of spiritual healing. Now, with *Healing
the Hurt*, everyone can understand the important skills needed by a Helper
to assure Workers find what they're looking for.

DOING THE WORK: Healing Our Body, Mind & Spirit by Getting
to Know the Self | By Jill Loree with Scott Wisler

Many of us have an inkling there can be more to life: that more meaningful moments are possible, and more satisfying experiences are attainable.
Well, we're right. And fortunately, the tools for bringing this about are not
really a secret. They're just not obvious. Herein lies the crux of the problem.
We must come to realize what we have not been willing or able to see before.

Truth be told, no one gets out of planet Earth alive. But we can come
out ahead by learning to make the best use of our time here. And that
starts the day we begin doing the work. So let's get at it.

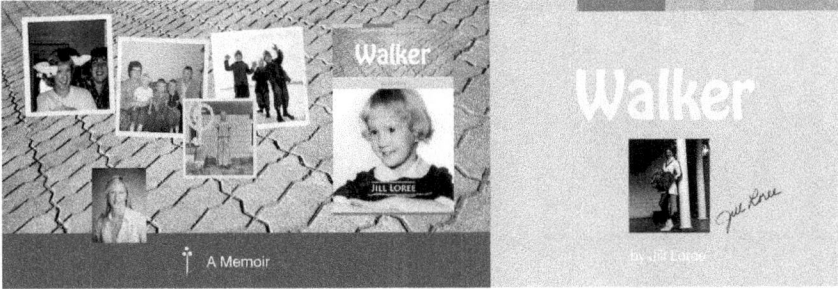

Walker
A Memoir

Walker is a memoir about one woman's spiritual journey to open her heart and develop compassion. Through it all, her own gumption would be her steady companion.

It starts out with a young girl raised in a singing Lutheran family where things looked good on the outside. But inside, Jill Loree was struggling. Later, she would "trudge the dreary road of happy destiny," as the AA Big Book puts it, getting sober at 26 and picking up only one white chip. That's not nothing, considering that most of Jill Loree's childhood memories are infused with her father's drinking. Her mother, on the other hand, had a controlling, co-dependent streak that wouldn't end.

Sounds dreary, right? In this spiritual memoir however, Jill Loree artfully lifts the story out of the ditch and finds the grace weaving between the lines. *Walker* also merges in a touch of poetry—her own, her sons' and even her Dad's—adding heart, depth and levity to the telling. Her gentle wit and brisk writing pace keeps things moving along. True to the title, there's no need to sit and stew in misery.

Today, Jill Loree's spiritual path is filled with the light of Christ, which is what she has discovered emerges from the core of one's being after clearing away the detritus accumulated in youth—just as the Pathwork Guide said it would. That's the deeper message she is now passionate about sharing, and which shines through in this warm telling of the story of her life.

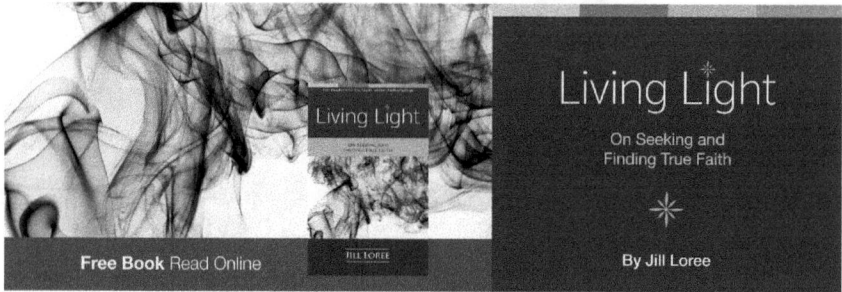

Living Light
On Seeking and Finding True Faith

What greater gift could we give ourselves than to wake up and bring forward the Christ consciousness that dwells within. To become a living light. Indeed, every time we listen for the truth, we will find the light of Christ within. And there is nothing greater for us to uncover than this, and to find true faith. For that's the moment we'll know there is truly nothing to fear.

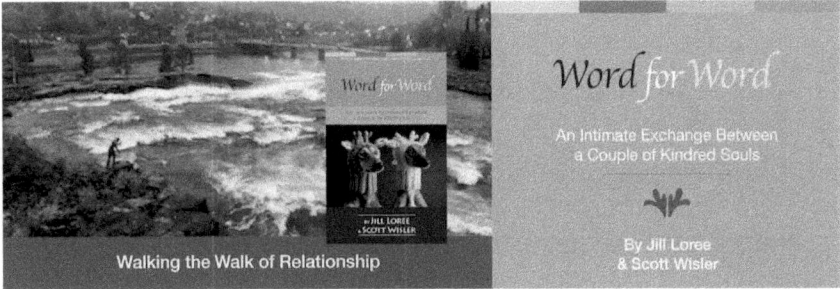

Walking the Walk of Relationship

Word for Word
An Intimate Exchange Between
a Couple of Kindred Souls
By Jill Loree
& Scott Wisler

Word for Word
An Intimate Exchange Between
a Couple of Kindred Souls

By Jill Loree
and Scott Wisler

What does it really look like, not just to talk the talk, but also to walk the walk of a spiritual path?

Surprisingly insightful and at times pretty funny, *Word for Word* is a unique collection of text and email messages written back and forth between a couple of died-in-the-wool spiritual seekers, Jill and Scott, as they walked head-long into a new relationship that would prove lasting.

Typos and punctuation have been cleaned up to aid readability, but believe it or not, nothing has been added or subtracted nor has anything been tweaked so the two don't look too strange. You'll see.

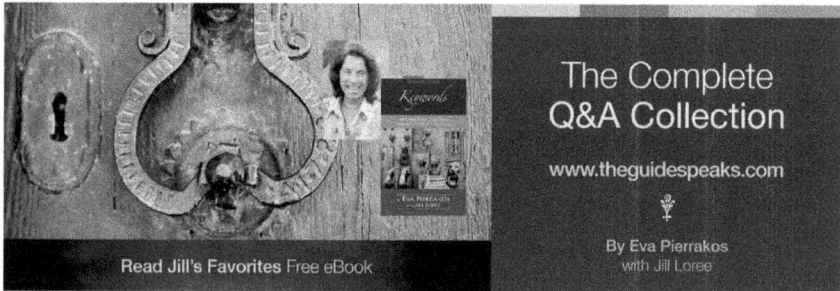

The Guide Speaks
The Complete Q&A Collection

By Eva Pierrakos
with Jill Loree

On *The Guide Speaks,* Jill Loree opens up this fascinating collection of thousands of Q&As answered by the Pathwork Guide, all arranged alphabetically by topic. This website includes hard-hitting questions asked about fears, hate, anger, health, relationships and so much more.

Jill Loree has combined her favorite questions about religion, Jesus Christ, the Bible, reincarnation, the Spirit World, death, prayer and meditation, and God into a single "Best Of" collection. You can read this collection online or download *Keywords: Answers to Key Questions Asked of the Pathwork® Guide.*

"There are so many questions you need to ask, personal and general ones. In the end they become one and the same. The lectures I am called upon to deliver are also answers to unspoken questions, questions that arise out of your inner yearning, searching, and desires to know and to be in truth. They arise out of your willingness to find divine reality, whether this attitude exists on the conscious or unconscious level.

But there are other questions that need to be asked deliberately on the active, outer, conscious level in order to fulfill the law. For only when you knock can the door be opened; only when you ask can you be given. This is a law."

– The Pathwork Guide in Q&A #250

www.theguidespeaks.com

Brought to you by your friends at Phoenesse®

phoeneſſe®
FIND YOUR TRUE YOU.

www.ingramcontent.com/pod-product-compliance
Lightning Source LLC
Chambersburg PA
CBHW070205060426
42445CB00033B/1546